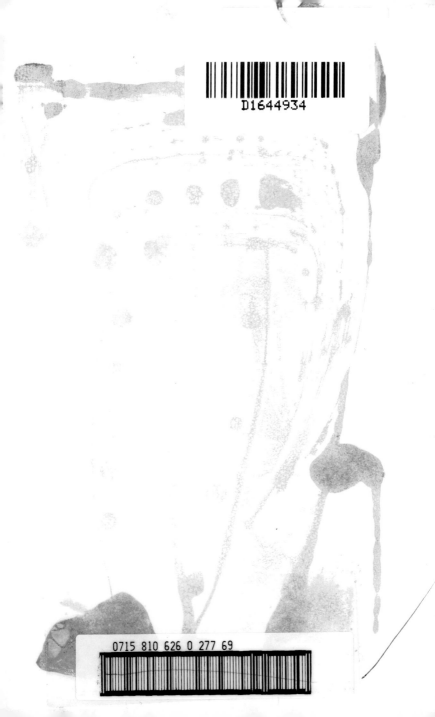

D1644934

THE
COUNTRY DANCE BOOK

PARTS III & IV

THE

COUNTRY DANCE BOOK

PARTS III & IV

DESCRIBED BY

CECIL J. SHARP

AND

GEORGE BUTTERWORTH.

Republished by
EP Publishing Limited
British Book Centre Inc.
1975

Republished 1975 by EP Publishing Limited
East Ardsley, Wakefield
Yorkshire, England
and
British Book Centre, Inc.
996 Lexington Ave.
New York, N.Y., USA

This is a reprint of Part III, first published in 1912, and Part IV,
first published in 1916. Both parts were originally published by
Novello & Company Limited

Corrections and additions

A printed list of corrections and additions, covering Parts II–VI,
has been discovered. It was published by Novello and Company,
Limited, and is undated. The items pertaining to Parts II, III and
IV are reproduced at the end of this book.

Copyright © 1975 EP Publishing Limited

ISBN 0 7158 1062 6 (UK)
ISBN 0 8277 3267 8 (USA)

793. 3194'2
SHA

ep

Please address all enquiries to EP Publishing Limited
(address as above)

Printed in Great Britain by
The Scolar Press Limited, Ilkley, Yorkshire

The English Dancing Master:

OR,

Plaine and easie Rules for the Dancing of Country Dances, with the Tune to each Dance.

mark. 1912

LONDON,

Printed by *Thomas Harper,* **and are to be sold by** *John Playford,* **at his Shop** **in the Inner** Temple neere the Church doore. 1651

THE

COUNTRY DANCE BOOK

PART III.

CONTAINING

THIRTY-FIVE COUNTRY DANCES

FROM

THE ENGLISH DANCING MASTER

(1650—1670)

DESCRIBED BY

CECIL J. SHARP

AND

GEORGE BUTTERWORTH.

LONDON:

NOVELLO AND COMPANY, Ltd.

1912.

CONTENTS.

PAGE

N<small>OTATION</small>—*contd.*

THE DANCE.

THE ROOM.

THE following diagram is a ground plan of the room in which the dances are supposed to take place.

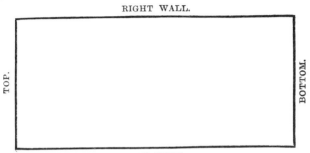

A diagram, showing the initial disposition of the dancers, will be printed with the notation of each dance, and will be so placed that its four sides correspond with the four sides of the room as depicted in the above plan. That is, the upper and lower sides of the diagram will represent, respectively, the right and left walls of the room; its left and right sides the top and bottom.

In Playford's time, the top of the room was often called "the Presence," alluding to the dais upon which the spectators were seated. The expression "facing the Presence" means, therefore, facing up, *i.e.*, toward the top of the room; while "back to the Presence" means facing down, toward the bottom of the room.

THE MUSIC.

The several strains of each dance-air will be marked in the music-book and in the notation by means of capital letters,

A, B, C, etc. When a strain is played more than once in a
Part it will be marked A1, B1, C1, etc., on its first performance, and A2, B2, C2, A3, B3, etc., in subsequent repetitions.

It will be found that most dances in this collection are divided
into two or more Parts. John Essex quaintly but aptly
likened these divisions to " the several verses of songs upon
the same tune."

In non-progressive dances, the division is made merely for
the sake of clearness in description ; the Parts are intended
to follow on without pause.

When, however, a progressive movement occurs in one or
other of the figures of a Part, that Part must be repeated as
often as the dancers decree. The usual practice is to repeat
the Part until the leader has returned to his original place at
the top of the General Set.

Progressive figures will, as heretofore, be marked as such in
the notation ; while the Parts in which they occur will be
headed " Whole-Set," " Duple Minor-Set," etc., according
to the nature of the progression.

THE STEPS.

Country Dance steps always fall on the first and middle
beats of the bar, whether the time be simple or compound.
When the step itself is a compound one, that is, when it consists of more than one movement, the accented movement
always falls upon the beginning of the beat.

The following abbreviations will be used in the music
diagrams : r. = right-foot ; l. = left-foot ; h. = hop ; f.t. =
feet-together ; $\cap$ = spring.

WALKING-STEP.

This is the springy walking-step described in Part 1 (p. 24).
The ball of the foot should take the ground before the heel.

In the notation this step will be called :—

w.s. (walking-step).

Running-Step.

A bounding or slow running step, executed upon the ball of the foot, with a moderate amount of spring, and with limbs relaxed. The arms, held loosely, should be slightly bent at the elbows, and allowed to swing naturally, forward and backward, in rhythm with the movements of the feet.

In the notation this step will be called : —

r.s. (running-step).

Skipping-Step.

This is a step and hop first on one foot and then on the other. The hop is made forward rather than up, and should raise the body as little as possible. When the steps are long and the motion rapid, the hop should be scarcely perceptible.

The accent is on the step, which must fall, therefore, on the beginning of the beat. The hop falls on the last quarter, or the last third of the beat, according as the latter is simple or compound, thus :—

In the notation this step will be called :—

sk.s. (skipping-step).

The Slip.

This, like the preceding, is a compound step. It is used in moving sideways along the straight, or around a circle, the dancer facing at right angles to the line of motion.

The performer stands with feet apart. If moving, say, to the left, a low spring is made off the left foot and the weight of the body transferred to the right foot, which alights close to the spot just vacated by the left foot. The left foot then falls to the ground, a foot or more to the side, a spring is again made off it, with a side thrust imparted by the right foot, and the movements are repeated. The legs are thus alternately opening and closing, scissor fashion.

The accent falls on the foot off which the spring is made, that is, the right or left, according as the motion is toward the right or left, thus :—

The slip is used in ring movements and whenever the dancers are directed to move sideways, or " slip " to right or left.

This step will be marked in the notation:—

sl.s. (slip-step).

THE DOUBLE-HOP.

This is sometimes used in ring movements, as an alternative to the preceding step. It is a variant of the Slip, in which the feet, instead of taking the ground one after the other, alight together, about six inches apart. The movement is, therefore, a series of jumps or double-hops.

THE SINGLE.

This consists of two movements. A step forward, or to the side, is made with one foot, say, the right, and the weight of the body supported upon it. The left foot, heel raised and toe touching the ground, is then drawn up and the heel placed in the hollow of the right foot (one bar).

As the left foot is dragged towards the right, the body is raised upon the instep of the right foot, and lowered as the

feet come together. These movements are shown in the
following diagram :—

$$\frac{2}{2} \quad \text{♩}_{\text{l.}} \quad \text{♩}_{\text{f.t.}} \quad | \quad \text{OR} \quad \frac{6}{8} \quad \text{♩.}_{\text{r.}} \quad \text{♩.}_{\text{f.t.}} \quad |$$

THE DOUBLE.

The double is three steps, forward or backward, followed
by " feet-together," thus :—

$$\frac{2}{2} \quad \text{o}_{\text{l.}} \quad \text{♩}_{\text{r.}} \quad | \quad \text{♩}_{\text{l.}} \quad \text{♩}_{\text{f.t.}} \quad | \quad \text{OR} \quad \frac{6}{8} \quad \text{♩.}_{\text{r}} \quad \text{♩.}_{\text{l.}} \quad | \quad \text{♩.}_{\text{r.}} \quad \text{♩.}_{\text{f.t.}} \quad |$$

THE JUMP.

The dancer, standing with feet parallel and close together,
springs off both feet and alights upon both feet. The knees
must not be bent.

THE RISE.

The dancer, standing as in the preceding figure, rises on
to the toes of both feet, rests there a moment, and then
lowers the heels to the ground.

THE FIGURES.

In the description of the following figures and, later on,
in the dance notations, many technical expressions will be
used. These will now be defined.

When two dancers, standing side by side, are directed to
" take hands," they are to join inside hands ; that is, the
right hand of one with the left of the other, if the two face
the same way ; and right hands or left hands, if they face in
opposite directions. If they are directed to take or give
right or left hands they are to join right with right, or left
with left.

To " cross hands " the man takes the right and left hands of the woman with, respectively, his right and left hands, the right hands being held above the left.

When two dancers face one another and are directed to take " both hands," they are to join right with left, and left with right.

To pass " by the right" is to pass right shoulder to right shoulder ; " by the left," left shoulder to left shoulder.

When a woman's path crosses that of a man's, the man must always allow the woman to pass first and in front of him.

When two dancers change places they should, unless otherwise directed, pass each other by the right.

When one dancer is told to " lead " another, the two join right or left hands according as the second dancer stands on the right or left hand of the leader.

To " cast off " is to turn outward and dance outside the General Set.

To " cast up " or " cast down " is to move up or down outside the General Set.

To " fall " hither or thither is to dance backwards ; to " lead," or " move," is to dance forwards.

To make a " half-turn " is to turn through half a circle and face in the opposite direction.

To make a " whole turn " means that the dancer revolves on his axis through a complete circle.

The disposition of the dancers is said to be " proper " when men and women are on their own sides; and " improper " when the men are on the women's side and the women on the men's.

In dances or figures in which two couples only are engaged, the terms " contrary woman " and " contrary man " are used to denote the woman or man other than the partner.

The terms " clockwise " and " counter-clockwise " are self-explanatory and refer to the direction of circular movements.

FIGURE 1.

Turn Single.

The dancer moves round in a small circle, clockwise (unless otherwise directed), taking four small walking- or running-steps, beginning with the right foot (two bars).

When the turn is to be made counter-clockwise, the first step is taken with the left foot.

FIGURE 2.

The Set.

This is a formal movement of courtesy, addressed by one dancer to another or, more frequently, by two dancers to each other, simultaneously. It consists of a single diagonally to the right, followed by a single diagonally to the left (two bars), thus:—

FIGURE 3.

In certain dances four instead of two bars are allotted to the Set. This may simply be an abbreviation or misprint for Set-and-turn-single; or it may bear a literal interpretation, in which case it is, perhaps, advisable to interpolate the Honour (Fig. 12, p. 14) after each single, thus:—

Whenever Set-and-honour occurs in the text, performers may either execute it in the way just described, or substitute Set-and-turn-single.

FIGURE 4.

The Side.

The dancer moves forward a double (w.s. or r.s.) obliquely to the right, makes a half-turn, counter-clockwise, and retraces his steps, thus :—

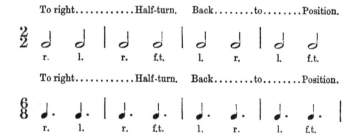

Sometimes, but very rarely, one only of the two movements is performed. In that event, the expression " side to the right," or " side to the left," is used.

FIGURE 5.

Arm with the Right.

Two performers, usually partners, meet, link right arms, swing round clockwise, separate, and fall back to places (r.s.) (four bars).

FIGURE 6.

Arm with the Left.

This is the same as the preceding movement except that the dancers link left instead of right arms, and swing round counter-clockwise instead of clockwise.

FIGURE 7.

ALL LEAD UP A DOUBLE AND FALL BACK A DOUBLE.

Couples stand in column formation, facing up. Each man then leads his partner up a double and, without turning or releasing hands, falls back a double (four bars). Dancers should begin each movement forward and backward, with outside feet.

FIGURE 8.

ALL LEAD UP A DOUBLE, CHANGE HANDS AND LEAD BACK A DOUBLE.

All lead up a double as in the preceding figure. They then release hands, make a half-turn, face downwards, and lead a double back to places (four bars).

FIGURE 9.

ALL MOVE UP A DOUBLE AND FALL BACK A DOUBLE.

Couples face up in column formation and, without handing, move up a double, and fall back a double to places (four bars).

In this and the two preceding figures, the dancers may bend or dive forward with a slight bowing movement as they take the first two steps up. This is frequently done by traditional dancers, especially when the running-step is used; and it is a very effective addition when properly executed, *i.e.*, without exaggeration.

FIGURE 10.

HANDS-TWO, HANDS-THREE, HANDS-FOUR, ETC.

Two or more dancers, as directed, join hands, dance round in a ring clockwise, facing centre, make one complete circuit, separate, and return to places (four bars).

If more or less than one circuit is to be made, specific instructions to that effect will be given in the notation, *e.g.*, half-way round, once-and-a-half round, etc. In the absence of any such directions it is to be understood that one complete circuit is to be danced.

The performers should clasp hands firmly, lean outward, and not dance too daintily. When the movement is followed by a repetition in the reverse direction, the dancers, without releasing hands, should stamp with both feet on the first beat of the second movement.

Occasionally, this figure is performed facing outward, that is, with backs turned toward the centre. Whenever this occurs special instructions to that effect will be given in the notation.

FIGURE 11.

The Turn.

Two dancers face each other, join both hands, swing round clockwise, separate, and return to places (two bars).

When four bars of the music are allotted to the movement, two complete circuits may be made.

In swinging, each performer should place both feet together, clasp hands firmly, and lean outward as in the ring movement.

FIGURE 12.

The Honour.

This, like the Set, is a formal movement of courtesy addressed by one dancer to another, or by two dancers to each other simultaneously.

In making the honour, the woman curtseys, and the man bows and, if he is wearing one, raises his hat.

The old custom was for partners to honour each other at the beginning and at the close of each dance.

FIGURE 13.

HALF-POUSETTE.

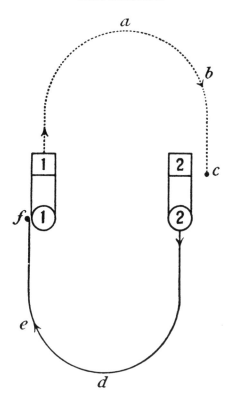

This is performed by two adjacent couples, usually the first and second.

Each man faces his partner and takes her by both hands. The arms must be held out straight, and very nearly shoulder high.

First man, pushing his partner before him, moves four steps along dotted line to *a*, and then falls back four steps along the line *a b c* into the second couple's place, pulling his partner after him.

Simultaneously, second man, pulling his partner after him, falls back four steps along unbroken line to *d*, and then moves forward four steps along the line *d e f* into the first couple's place (four bars).

The above movement is called the half-pousette, and is, of course, a progressive figure.

When the half-pousette is followed by a repetition of the same movement, each couple describing a complete circle or ellipse, the figure is called the whole-pousette.

FIGURE 14.

First Couple Casts Off into Second Place.

First man turns outward to his left and casts off and down, outside second man, into the second place; while first woman turns outward to her right and casts off and down into the second place. Simultaneously, second man and second woman slip up into the first place. This is a progressive figure.

FIGURE 15.

Back-to-Back.

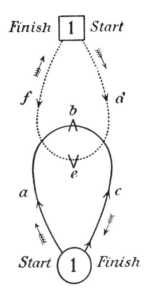

First man and first woman face each other and move forward, the man along the line *a b*, the woman along the dotted line *d e*. They pass by the right, move round each other, back to back, and fall back to places, the man along the line *b c*, the woman along the dotted line *e f* (four bars).

The arrow heads in the diagram show the positions of the dancers at the end of each bar and point in the directions in which they are facing. The arrows outside the lines show the direction in which the dancers move.

FIGURE 16.

WHOLE-GIP FACING CENTRE.

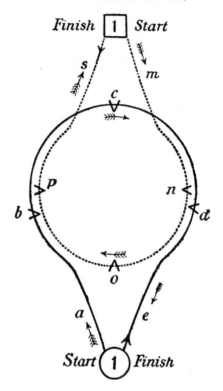

First man moves forward along line *a*, dances round circle *b c d*, keeping his face toward the centre, and falls back along line *d e* to place; while first woman dances along dotted line *m*, moves round circle *n o p*, keeping her face toward the centre, and falls back along dotted line *p s* to place (four bars).

The arrows and arrow heads have the same significations as in the preceding figure.

FIGURE 17.

WHOLE-GIP FACING OUTWARD.

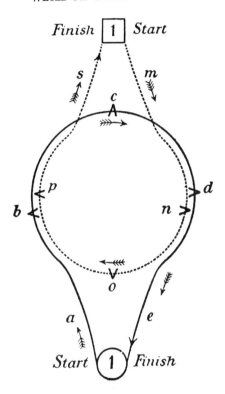

First man moves along line *a* and dances round circle *b c d*, facing outward, to place; while first woman moves along dotted line *m*, dances round circle *n o p*, facing outward, and moves along dotted line *p s* to place (four bars).

FIGURE 18.

Right-Hands-Across.

This is performed by four dancers, usually the first and second couples.

First man and second woman join right hands, while second man and first woman do the same. Holding hands, chin high, the four dancers dance round, clockwise, to places, all facing in the direction in which they are moving.

FIGURE 19.

Left-Hands-Across.

This is very similar to the preceding figure, the dancers joining left instead of right hands and dancing round counter-clockwise instead of clockwise.

It is to be understood that in both of these figures the dancers make one complete circuit unless specific instructions to the contrary are given.

THE HEY.

The Hey may be defined as the rhythmical interlacing in serpentine fashion of two groups of dancers, moving in single file and in opposite directions.

The figure assumes different forms according to the disposition of the dancers. These varieties, however, fall naturally into two main types according as the track described by the dancers—disregarding the deviations made by them in passing one another—is (1) a straight line, or (2) the perimeter of a closed figure, circle or ellipse.

The second of these species, as the simpler of the two, will be first explained.

FIGURE 20.

THE CIRCULAR HEY.

In the analysis that follows the circle will, for the sake of convenience, be used throughout to represent the track described by the dancers in this form of the figure. In the round dance the track will, of course, be a true circle ; while in the square dance it will become one as soon as the movement has begun. On the other hand, in a longways dance, the formation will be elliptical rather than circular, but this will not affect the validity of the following explanation.

In the circular Hey the dancers, who must be even in number, are stationed, at equal distances, around the circumference of a circle, facing alternately in opposite directions, thus : —

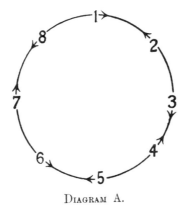

DIAGRAM A.

Odd numbers face and move round clockwise ; even numbers counter-clockwise. All move at the same rate and upon meeting, pass alternately by the right and left.

This progression is shown in the following diagram, the dotted and unbroken lines indicating the tracks described, respectively, by odd and even numbers. It will be seen that in every circuit the two opposing groups of dancers, odd and even, thread through each other twice; that is, there will be eight simultaneous passings, or "changes," as we will call them, in each complete circuit :—

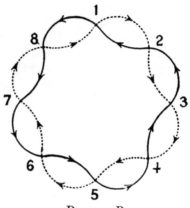

DIAGRAM B.

This movement is identical with that of the Grand Chain, except that in the familiar Lancers' figure the performers take hands, alternately right and left, as they pass; whereas, in the Country Dance Hey, "handing," as Playford called it, is the exception rather than the rule.

In this form the Hey presents no difficulty. No misconception can arise so long as (1) the initial dispositions of the pairs, and (2) the duration of the movement, measured by circuits or changes, are clearly defined. And instructions on these two points will always be given in the notation. It should be understood that, in the absence of directions to the contrary, the dancers are to pass each other without handing.

FIGURE 21.
Progressive Circular Hey.

Sometimes the Hey is danced progressively, the dancers beginning and ending the movement pair by pair, instead of simultaneously, as above described. This is effected in the following way :—

The first change is performed by one pair only, say Nos. 1 and 2 (see diagram A, Fig. 20) ; the second by two pairs, Nos. 1 and 3, and Nos. 2 and 8 ; the third, in like manner, by three pairs ; and the fourth by four pairs. At the conclusion of the fourth change Nos. 1 and 2 will be face to face, each having traversed half a circuit ; and all the dancers will be actively engaged, thus :—

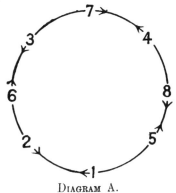

DIAGRAM A.

The movement now proceeds in the usual way. At the end of every complete circuit the position will be as follows :—

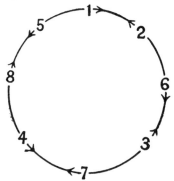

DIAGRAM B.

The figure is concluded in the following manner:—
Nos. 1 and 2, upon reaching their original places (see
diagram B), stop and remain neutral for the rest of the
movement. The others continue dancing until they reach
their proper places when they, in like manner, stop and
become neutral. This they will do pair by pair in the
following order, Nos. 3 and 8, 4 and 7, 5 and 6. The
initial and final movements thus occupy the same time,
i.e., four changes.

Whenever the progressive Hey occurs (1) the initial pair
will be named; and (2) the duration of the movement,
measured by changes or circuits, will be given in the notation.

FIGURE 22.

THE STRAIGHT HEY.

The dancers stand in a straight line at equi-distant stations,
alternately facing up and down, thus:—

DIAGRAM A.

Odd numbers face down; even numbers up. As in the
circular Hey the dancers move at an even rate, and pass each
other alternately by the right and left. The movement is
shown in diagram B, the dotted and unbroken lines indicating,
respectively, the upward and downward tracks described by
the dancers:—

DIAGRAM B.

From this diagram it will be seen that the movements of individual dancers are the same as those of the couples in a progressive Country Dance (duple minor-set), with this difference—that the neutrals, instead of remaining passive, reverse their directions by moving round a loop.

In the first change, all the dancers will be actively engaged in meeting and passing each other ; and there will be no neutrals. But in the second change, there will be two neutrals, Nos. 2 and 7, who will move, respectively, round the loops *a b* and *c d*. At the beginning of the third change, Nos. 2 and 7 re-enter the track and all the dancers pass, in pairs, as in the first change. By means of the terminal loops the track is converted into an endless path and, in this way, the continuous and characteristic rhythmic movement of the Hey is preserved.

When, therefore, the number of dancers is even, as in the above example, there will be in alternate rounds (1) no neutrals, and (2) two neutrals, one at each end.

The distribution, however, will be somewhat different when the number of dancers is uneven, as the following diagram will show :—

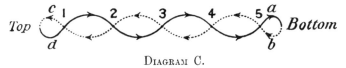

DIAGRAM C.

Odd numbers face down ; even numbers up. No. 5, having no partner, is neutral in the first change. In the second change, No. 2 will be neutral at the other end. In every change, therefore, there will be one neutral, alternately at the top and bottom.

When this variation is performed by three dancers only, we have the form in which the Hey occurs most frequently in the Country Dance. For this reason it will, perhaps, be advisable to describe this particular form in detail.

FIGURE 23.

The Hey for Three.

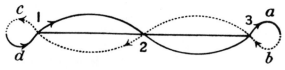

Nos. 1 and 3 face down; No. 2 up. The figure is performed in six changes, thus:—

(1.)   Nos. 1 and 2 pass by the right; while No. 3 moves round the loop *a b*.

(2.)   Nos. 1 and 3 pass by the left; while No. 2 moves round the loop *c d*.

(3.)   Nos. 2 and 3 pass by the right; while No. 1 moves round the loop *a b*.

This completes the first half of the movement, which is called the *half-hey*. Nos. 1 and 3 have changed ends, while No. 2 is in his original station.

The second half of the figure proceeds as follows: —

(4.)   Nos. 1 and 2 pass by the left; while No. 3 moves round the loop *c d*.

(5.)   Nos. 1 and 3 pass by the right; while No. 2 moves round the loop *a b*.

(6.)   Nos. 2 and 3 pass by the left; while No. 1 moves round the loop *c d*.

This completes the *whole-hey*, as it is called, and leaves the dancers in their original stations.

The above is, presumably, the correct way in which this figure should be performed. Whether or not it was so danced in the 17th century there is, apparently, no evidence to prove. Hogarth, however, gives a diagram in his *Analysis of Beauty*, which shows—though not very clearly—how the Hey for three was danced at that period, *i.e.*, 1753; while Wilson (*The Analysis of Country Dancing*, 1811) describes the way in which this figure was performed in his day; and there is, of course, the Hey of the present-day Morris Dance (see *Morris Book* i., 70). These three forms all differ, and not one of them is the same as that above described. The differences are, however, comparatively unimportant ; in all essential points they accord. Each one—to use Hogarth's words—" is a cypher of S's, a number of serpentine lines interlacing or intervolving each other."

For the information of those interested in the subject, a diagram showing the way in which the Hey for three was danced in the early years of the last century, will now be given. Except that the tracks of the three dancers are differentiated from one another by means of varied lines, the diagram is an exact reproduction of that printed in Wilson's *Complete System :—*

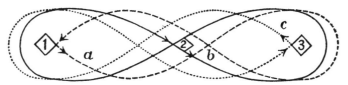

No. 1 moves along the broken line *a*; No. 2 along the line *b*; and No. 3 along the dotted line *c*.

The Straight Hey is sometimes performed progressively. It is unnecessary, however, to describe in detail the way in which this is effected, because, in principle, the method is the same as that already explained in Fig. 21. (see p. 22).

Playford, in his descriptions of the dances, makes frequent use of the expressions "Single Hey" and "Double Hey." It is difficult to say with certainty what he meant by these terms, because he uses them very loosely. Apparently, they are identical with what we have called the Straight and Circular Hey. As, however, this interpretation is somewhat speculative, I have, with some reluctance, substituted the terms used in the text, which are self-explanatory and free from ambiguity.

NOTATION.

CATCHING OF QUAILS.

Round for eight ; in three parts (4th Ed. 1670).

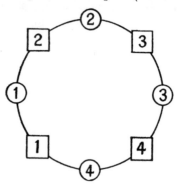

MUSIC.		MOVEMENTS.
		FIRST PART.
A	1—8	Hands-all, eight slips clockwise, and eight slips counter-clockwise to places.
B1	1—2	First man moves in front of his partner, and faces her (r.s.).
	3—4	First man moves back a double into the centre, followed by his partner (r.s.).
	5—8	Second couple does the same.
B2	1—4	Third couple does the same.
	5—8	Fourth couple does the same.
		All the men are now in the middle, facing their partners.

CATCHING OF QUAILS—*continued.*

MUSIC.		MOVEMENTS.
		SECOND PART.
A	1—4	Partners side (r.s.).
	5—8	That again.
B1	1—2	First man shakes his partner by the right hand three times, on the first and middle beats of the first bar, and on the first beat of the second bar.
	3—4	First man turns his partner half-way round with his right hand, and changes places with her.
	5—8	Second couple does the same.
B2	1—4	Third couple does the same.
	5—8	Fourth couple does the same.
		All the women are now in the middle, facing their partners.
		THIRD PART.
A	1—4	Partners arm with the right.
	5—8	Partners arm with the left.
B1	1—2	First man taps his partner's right foot with his right foot three times, on the first and middle beats of the first bar, and on the first beat of the second bar.
	3—4	First woman moves out into her original place (r.s.).
	5—8	Second couple does the same.
B2	1—4	Third couple does the same.
	5—8	Fourth couple does the same.

IF ALL THE WORLD WERE PAPER.

Round for eight; in three parts (1st Ed. 1650).

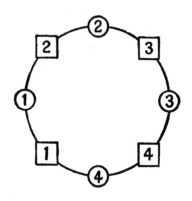

MUSIC.		MOVEMENTS.
		FIRST PART.
A1	1—4	All take hands, move forward a double, and fall back a double to places (r.s.).
	5—8	Partners set and turn single.
A2	1—8	All that again.
A3	1—2	First and third men change places (r.s.).
	3—4	First and third women change places (r.s.).
	5—8	Circular-hey (Fig. 20, p. 21), to places, two changes, partners facing each other (sk.s.).
A4	1—8	Second and fourth couples do the same.

IF ALL THE WORLD WERE PAPER—*continued.*

MUSIC.		MOVEMENTS.
		SECOND PART.
A1	1—4	Partners side (r.s.).
	5 – 8	Partners set and turn single.
A2	1—8	All that again.
A3	1—2	First and third couples move forward a double and meet (r.s.)
	8—4	First man leads third woman between second man and second woman; while third man leads first woman between fourth man and fourth woman (r.s.).
	5—6	All four cast off to their respective places (sk.s).
	7 · 8	First and third men turn their partners.
A4	1—8	Second and fourth couples do the same.
		THIRD PART.
A1	1—4	Partners arm with the right.
	5—8	Partners set and turn single.
A2	1—4	Partners arm with the left.
	5—8	Partners set and turn single.
A3	1—2	First man and third woman change places; while first woman and third man do the same (r.s.).
	3—4	First and third men change places with their partners (r.s.).
	5—8	Circular-hey (Fig. 20, p. 21), handing, to places; two changes, each man facing the contrary woman (sk.s.).
A4	1—8	Second and fourth couples do the same.

UP TAILS ALL.

Round for as many as will; in four parts (1st Ed., 1650).

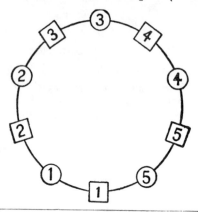

MUSIC.		MOVEMENTS.
		FIRST PART.
A1	1—4	All take hands, move forward a double, and fall back a double to places (r.s.).
	5—8	Partners set and turn single.
A2	1—8	All that again.
		SECOND PART.
A1	1—4	First man and first woman lead between second man and second woman, separate, cast off, and meet each other in front of second couple (r.s.).
	5—8	First man and first woman clap hands, arm with the right, pass on, and face third couple.
		This movement is repeated until the first couple has passed all the other couples. The second couple then does the same; then the third, and so on.

UP TAILS ALL—*continued.*

Music.		Movements.
		THIRD PART.
A1	1 —4	As in Second Part.
	5 —8	First and second couples clap hands and right-hands-across (sk.s.), first couple passing on to third couple.
		Movement repeated as in Second Part.
		FOURTH PART.
A1	1—4	As in Second Part.
	5—8	First and second couples clap hands and hands-four, first couple passing on to third couple.
		Movement repeated as in Second Part.

Parts 2, 3 *and* 4 *may be done progressively by all the couples in the usual way (duple minor-set), the first couple's place being treated as the top place of a longways dance, and the last couple's place as the bottom.*

WINIFRED'S KNOT, or OPEN THE DOOR TO THREE.

Round for as many as will ; in three parts (2nd Ed. 1652).

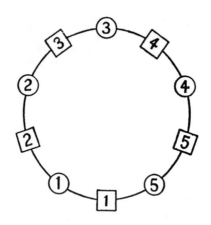

Music.		Movements.
		First Part.
A1	1—4	Hands-all, eight slips clockwise.
	5—6	All turn single.
A2	1—4	Hands-all, eight slips counter-clockwise to places.
	5—6	All turn single.
A3 (repeated as many times as there are couples)		
	1—4	Men move forward a double, meet, and fall back a double to places (r.s.).

WINIFRED'S KNOT—*continued.*

Music.	Movements.
	FIRST PART—*contd.*
5—6	Each man passes outside the woman on his left, and moves into the next man's place (r.s.). These two movements are repeated until the men have returned to their places.
A4 (repeated as many times as there are couples)	
1—4	Women move forward a double, meet, and fall back a double to places (r.s.).
5—6	Each woman passes outside the man on her right, and moves into the next woman's place (r.s.). These two movements are repeated until the women have returned to their places.
	SECOND PART.
A1 1—4	Partners side (r.s.).
5—6	All turn single.
A2 1—6	All that again.
A3 1—6	Same as in A4 (First Part).
A4 1—6	Same as in A3 (First Part).
	THIRD PART.
A1 1—4	Partners arm with the right.
5—6	All turn single.
A2 1—4	Partners arm with the left.
5—6	All turn single.
A3 1—6	As in A3, First Part.
A4 1—6	As in A4, First Part.

CHELSEA REACH.
Square for eight; in three parts (3rd Ed., **1665**).

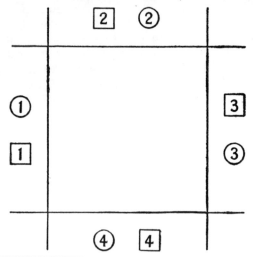

Music		Movements.

First Part.*

A1	1—4	All move forward a double and fall back a double to places (r.s.).
	5—8	Partners set-and-honour (Fig. 3, p. 11).
B1	1—4	All face outward. Partners lead out a double, and fall back a double to places (r.s.).
	5—8	Partners set-and-honour.
A2	1—2	Second and fourth couples meet and stand back-to-back (r.s.). Simultaneously, first man and first woman change places, move forward and come face to face, respectively, with fourth man and second woman (sk.s.); while third man and third woman do the same and face, respectively, second man and fourth woman.

* See note at end of dance.

CHELSEA REACH—*continued.*

Music.	Movements.
3—4	Second couple, first woman and third man hands-four, half-way round; while the other four do the same.
Bar 5	Second and fourth men give right hands to their partners and change places with them; while first man does the same with third woman, and third man with first woman (sk.s.).
6—8	First and fourth men turn with the left hand, and move back to their original places; while second and third men, first and second women, and third and fourth women do the same (sk.s.).
B2 1—8	Same movement as in A2, first and third couples meeting in the middle.

SECOND PART.

A1 1—4	Partners side (r.s.).
5—8	Partners set-and-honour.
B1 1—8	All that again.
A2 1—2	Each man takes his partner by both hands and pushes her backward into the middle (r.s.).
3—4	Partners change places (r.s.).
5—8	Partners change places. The women right-hands-across half-way round; while the men dance half-way round, counter-clockwise, outside them (sk.s.). The couples are now in opposite places.
B2 1—8	The movement continued as in A2 to places, the women setting the men in the middle, the men giving left-hands-across, and the women dancing round, clockwise, outside them.

CHELSEA REACH—*continued.*

Music.		Movements.
		Third Part.
A1	1—4	Partners arm with the right.
	5—8	Partners set-and-honour.
B1	1—4	Partners arm with the left.
	5—8	Partners set-and-honour.
A2	1—4	Each man, taking the woman on his left by the left hand, leads out a double, changes hands and leads back a double (r.s.).
	5—8	Circular-hey with hands (Fig. 20, p. 21), half-way round, each man giving his right hand to the woman on his left (sk.s.). Each man is now face to face with the woman he led out.
B2	1—8	Same as A2 to places.

Playford's description of the First Part is so obscure, that the editors would probably have omitted the dance altogether, had it not been such an interesting and beautiful one. The interpretation given above depends on the supposition (paralleled only in " Fain I Would ") that the women throughout the dance stand on the left of their partners; this peculiarity has not been preserved in the text, as it makes no difference to the form of the dance, and would merely perplex the performers. There is a further difficulty in that the figures do not properly fit the music; this has been obviated by omitting one of the movements (a " turn ") given by Playford.

Under these circumstances the editors make no claim to have found a final solution. The following interpretation, which is put forward as

CHELSEA REACH—*continued.*

Music.		Movements
		an alternative, does not presuppose the unusual disposition of the dancers alluded to above, though in other respects it is perhaps less probable than the version given in the text.

First Part.
(Alternative Version.)

Music.		Movements
A1	1—8	As above.
B1	1—8	As above.
A2	1—4	Second and fourth couples meet and stand back-to-back. Simultaneously, first man and first woman change places, turn off to their right and come face to face, respectively, with second woman and fourth man; while third man and third woman do the same and face, respectively, fourth woman and second man (r.s.).
	5—6	Second couple, first man and third woman hands-four, half-way round; while the other four do the same.
	7—8	Second and fourth men give right hands to their partners and change places; while first man does the same with third woman, and third man with first woman (r.s.).
B2	1—4	Second couple, first man and third woman left-hands-across; while the other four do the same.
	5—8	Each man turns his partner twice round and all fall into their original places.
A3 & B3		Same movement as in A2 and B2, first and third couples meeting in the middle.
		In this version the tune must be played three times instead of twice.

FAIN I WOULD.

Square for eight; in three parts (1st Ed. 1650).

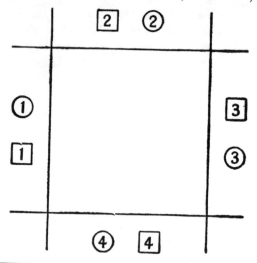

Music.		Movements.
		FIRST PART.
A1	1—4	Partners lead out a double, change hands, and lead in to places (r.s.).
	5—6	Each man takes the woman on his left by both hands, and changes places with her.
	7—8	First man and first woman, third man and third woman, second man and fourth woman, and second woman and fourth man, change places in like manner.
A2	1—4	Each man leads out the woman on his right a double, changes hands and leads in a double (r.s.).

FAIN I WOULD—*continued.*

Music.		Movements.
		First Part—*contd.*
	5—8	Same as in A1.
B1	1—2	First and third couples move forward and meet (r.s.)
	3—4	First couple with fourth man and second woman take hands and fall back a double ; while the other four do likewise (r.s.).
	5—8	First man and third woman arm with the right and fall into the second place, third man and first woman doing the same and falling into the fourth place ; while fourth man and second woman arm on the outside and fall into the first place, second man and fourth woman doing the same and falling into the third place.
		All the women are now on the left of the men.
B2	1—8	Same movements as in B1, second man and fourth woman meeting fourth man and second woman in the middle, and all arming with the left.
		All are now in their original places.
		Second Part.
A1	1—4	Partners side (r.s.).
	5—8	Same as in A1, First Part.
A2	1—4	Each man sides with the woman on his right (r.s.).
	5—8	Same as in A1, First Part.

FAIN I WOULD—*continued.*

Music.		Movements.
		SECOND PART—*contd.*
B1	1—4	First man turns out to his right and, followed by second woman, returns to his place; while third man, followed by fourth woman, does the same. Simultaneously, first woman turns out to her left and, followed by fourth man, returns to her place; while third woman, followed by second man, does the same (r.s.).
	5—8	First couple with fourth man and second woman hands-four; while the other four do the same.
B2	1—4	Second man turns out to his right and, followed by third woman, returns to his place; while fourth man, followed by first woman, does the same. Simultaneously, second woman turns out to her left and, followed by first man, returns to her place; while fourth woman, followed by third man, does the same (r.s.).
	5—8	Second couple with first man and third woman hands-four; while the other four do the same.

FAIN I WOULD—*continued.*

Music.		Movements.

THIRD PART.

A1   1—4   Partners arm with the right.

         5—8   Same as in **A1**, First Part.

A2   1—4   Each man arms with the left the woman on his right.

         5—8   Same as in **A1**, First Part.

B1   1—2   First and third couples move forward and meet (r.s.).

         3—8   First and third couples hands-four, facing outward, once round, clockwise. Simultaneously, second and fourth couples hands-four round them, counter-clockwise. First man and third woman fall into the second place, third man and first woman into the fourth place, fourth man and second woman into the first place, and second man and fourth woman into the third place.

The women are now on the left of the men.

B2   1—8   Same movement as in **B1**, fourth man and second woman meeting second man and fourth woman in the middle.

All are now in their original places.

In this dance Playford directs that the women shall stand on the left of their partners. For simplicity's sake this unusual disposition has not been adhered to in the text, the alteration making no difference to the form of the dance

HYDE PARK.

Square for eight; in three parts (1st Ed. 1650).

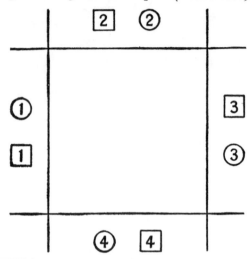

MUSIC.		MOVEMENTS.
		FIRST PART.
A	1—4	First and third couples move forward a double, meet, and fall back a double to places (w.s.).
	5—8	Second and fourth couples do the same.
B1	1—2	First man and first woman face and take both hands; while third man and third woman do the same.
	3—4	First and third couples slip sideways and meet.
	5—8	First man and third woman, taking both hands, slip between second man and second woman, separate, and cast off to places; while third man and first woman slip between fourth man and fourth woman, separate, and cast off to places.

HYDE PARK—*continued.*

Music.		Movements.
		FIRST PART—*contd.*
B2	1—8	Same movement as in B1, second and fourth couples slipping toward each other and meeting.
		SECOND PART.
A	1—8	Same as in First Part.
B1	1—2	Second man and second woman change places and, holding up right hands, make an arch; while fourth man and fourth woman do the same.
	3—8	First man and first woman face and pass each other by the right. The first man, going on the outside of the fourth couple, then passes under the arch and returns to the first woman's place; while the first woman, going outside the second couple, passes under the arch and returns to the first man's place. Simultaneously, the third man and third woman do the same (sk.s.).
B2	1—2	First man and first woman change places and, holding up right hands, make an arch; while third man and third woman do the same.
	3—8	Second man and second woman face, pass each other by the right, and then, doing the same as first man and first woman in B1, return to their proper places; while fourth man and fourth woman do likewise.

HYDE PARK—*continued.*

Music.		Movements.
		THIRD PART.
A	1—8	Same as in First Part.
B1	1—8	Each man moves forward on the inside of his partner, then on the outside of the next woman, and in this way passes round, counter-clockwise, to his place (sk.s.).
B2	1—8	Each woman moves forward on the inside of her partner, then on the outside of the next man, and in this way passes round, clockwise, to her place (sk.s.).

HUNSDON HOUSE.
Square for eight; in three parts (3rd Ed. 1665).

Music.	Movements.
	FIRST PART.
A 1—2	First and third couples move forward a double and meet. Simultaneously, second man and second woman face each other and fall back a double; while fourth man and fourth woman do the same (r.s.).
3—4	First man gives his right hand to third woman, and falls back with her into the second couple's place; while third man gives his right hand to first woman, and falls back with her into the fourth couple's place. Simultaneously, second man and fourth woman face each other, move forward and meet in the third couple's place, the fourth man and second woman doing the same in the first couple's place (r.s.).
	The women are now on the left of the men.

HUNSDON HOUSE—*continued.*

Music.	Movements.
	First Part—*contd.*
5—8	All that again, the second man and fourth woman meeting the fourth man and second woman, while the others fall back.
	All are now in their original places.
B1 1—4	First and third couples move forward a double (r.s.), meet, and turn single.
5—6	First and third men cross and move into third and first places (r.s.).
7—8	First and third women do the same (r.s.).
B2 1—8	Second and fourth couples do likewise.
B3 and **B4**	Same as in B1 and B2, to places.
	Second Part.
A 1—8	As in First Part.
B1 1—4	First and third couples move forward a double (r.s.), meet and stand back to back.
5—8	Hands-four, facing outward, half-way round, the first couple falling into third place, third couple into first place.
B2 1—8	Second and fourth couples do likewise.
B3 and **B4**	Same as in B1 and B2, to places.
	Third Part.
A 1—8	As in First Part.
B1 1—2	First and third couples move forward a double and meet (r.s.).
3—4	First and third men honour their partners.
5—8	Circular-hey (Fig. 20, p. 21), handing, two changes, each man facing the contrary woman (sk.s.).
	The couples have now changed places.
B2 1—8	Second and fourth couples do likewise.
B3 and **B4**	As in B1 and B2, to places, except that the men honour the contrary women, and partners face for the Hey.

ALTHEA.

For four ; in three parts (3rd Ed. 1665).

Music.		Movements.
		First Part.
A1	1—4	The two couples lead forward a double, meet, and fall back a double to places (r.s.).
	5—8	Partners set, thus: Spring on to right foot and hold up left foot, repeating with reverse feet; then jump three times with crossed feet.
A2	1—8	All that again.
B1	1—2	The two couples move forward a double and meet (r.s.).
	3—4	First man and second woman fall back a double to places; while first woman and second man cross over and change places (r.s.).
	5—8	Each man sets (as above) with the contrary woman.
B2	1—2	The two men and the two women move forward a double and meet (r.s.).
	3—4	First woman and second man fall back a double to places; while first man and second woman cross over and change places (r.s.).
	5—8	Partners set (as above).
B3	1—8	As in B1.
B4	1—8	As in B2 to places.

ALTHEA—*continued.*

Music.		Movements.
		SECOND PART.
A1	1—4	Partners side (r.s.).
	5—8	Partners set (as above).
A2	1—4	Each man sides with the contrary woman (r.s.).
	5—8	Each man sets (as above) with the contrary woman.
B1	1—4	First man casts off to his left, and, followed by his partner, returns to his place.
	5—8	First man and first woman set (as above).
B2	1—8	The second couple does the same.
		THIRD PART.
A1	1—4	Partners arm with the right.
	5—8	Partners set (as above).
A2	1—4	Men arm contrary women with the left.
	5—8	Each man sets (as above) with the contrary woman.
B1	1—2	First man and second woman move forward a double and meet (r.s.).
	3—8	First man and second woman stand back to back, take hands, and move round clockwise to places; while first woman and second man move round them in a circle, counter-clockwise, to places (r.s.).
B2	1—2	Second man and first woman move forward a double and meet (r.s.).
	3—8	Second man and first woman stand back to back, take hands and move round clockwise to places; while second woman and first man move round them in a circle, counter-clockwise, to places.

ARGEERS.

For four; in three parts (1st Ed. 1650).

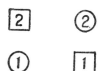

Music.		Movements.

FIRST PART.

A1 1—2 | The two couples move forward a double and meet (w.s.).

3—4 | First man takes second woman by both hands, moves two slips to his left and two slips back again; while second man does the same with first woman.

5—8 | Each man changes places with the contrary woman; whereupon partners turn once-and-a-half round and change places.

A2 1—8 | First man turns second woman once-and-a-half round to places; while second man does the same with the first woman. Then each man turns his partner.

B1 1—2 | First and second men cross over and change places (r.s.).

3—4 | First and second women do the same (r.s.).

5—8 | Partners set and turn single.

B2 1—2 | First and second women cross over and change places (r.s.).

3—4 | First and second men do the same (r.s.).

5—8 | Partners set and turn single.

ARGEERS—*continued.*

Music.		Movements.
		Second Part.
A1	1—4	First man leads second woman up a double and falls back a double; while second man leads first woman down a double and falls back a double (r.s.).
	5—8	Each man turns his partner.
A2	1—4	All fall back a double and move forward a double to places (r.s.).
	5—8	Partners set and turn single.
B1	1—4	Each man moves four slips to his right behind his partner, and four slips back again to his place; while each woman moves four slips to her left in front of her partner, and four slips back again to her place.
	5—8	Each man turns the contrary woman.
B2	1—4	The two women move forward a double, meet, and fall back a double to places (r.s.).
	5—8	The two men pass each other by the right, make a whole turn, counter-clockwise, pass each other by the right, and return to places (sk.s.).
		Third Part.
A1	1—4	First man, taking second woman by both hands, pushes her back, moves to his right and falls back into his partner's place; while second man does the same with first woman (r.s.).
	5—8	Partners set and turn single.

Music.		Movements.
		THIRD PART—*contd.*
A2	1 4	Same as A1 to places, moving to the left.
	5—8	Partners set and turn single.
B1	1—4	First man casts off to his left and, followed by his partner, returns to his place ; while second woman, followed by second man, casts off to her right and returns to her place (sk.s.).
	5—8	First woman casts off to her right and, followed by her partner, returns to her place ; while second man casts off to his left and does the same (sk.s.).
B2	1—4	Circular-hey (Fig. 20 p. 21), half-way round, two changes, each man facing the contrary woman (r.s.).
	5—8	Each man turns his partner ; all four face up and, standing in line, with hands joined, the second couple on the left, honour the Presence.

LADY IN THE DARK.

For four; in three parts (3rd Ed 1665).

Music.		Movements.
		FIRST PART.
A1	1—2	Couples move forward a double and meet (w.s.).
	3—4	All make a half-turn outward (men to their left, women to their right) and return to places (r.s.).
	5—6	Men change places (r.s.).
	7—8	Women change places (r.s.).
A2	1—8	All that again to places.
A3	1—4	The two men move forward a double, meet, fall back two steps, move forward two steps and meet again (r.s.).
	5—8	The two men arm with the right, and then, turning the contrary women with left hands, return to places (r.s.).
A4	1—4	The two women move forward a double, meet, fall back two steps, move forward two steps, and meet again (r.s.).
	5—8	The two women arm with the left and then, turning the contrary men with right hands, return to places (r.s.).

LADY IN THE DARK—*continued.*

Music.		Movements.
		SECOND PART.
A1	1—4	Each man sides with the contrary woman (r.s.).
	5—8	Each man Set-and-honour (Fig. 3, p. 11) with the contrary woman.
A2	1—4	Partners side (r.s.).
	5—8	Partners Set-and-honour.
A3	1—2	The two couples move forward a double and meet (w.s.).
	3—4	First man takes second woman by the right hand and falls back a double toward the Presence; while second man takes first woman by the right hand, faces the Presence and falls back a double (r.s.).
	5—6	First man and second woman change places with second man and first woman, the latter couple passing under the arms of the former (r.s.).
	7—8	Same again, first man and second woman passing under the arms of the other two (r.s.).
A4	1—2	Partners face, move forward a double and meet (w.s.).
	3—4	Partners, taking right hands, fall back a double, the first couple to the left wall, the second couple to the right wall (r.s.).
	5—6	First couple passes under the arms of second man and second woman, and changes places with them (r.s.).
	7—8	Second couple passes under the arms of first man and first woman, and changes places with them (r.s.).

LADY IN THE DARK—*continued.*

Music.		Movements.
		THIRD PART.
A1	1—4	Each man arms the contrary woman with the right.
	5—8	Each man Set-and-honour with the contrary woman.
A2	1—4	Partners arm with the left.
	5—8	Partners Set-and-honour.
A3	1—4	Circular-hey (Fig. 20, p. 21), with hands, two changes, each man facing the contrary woman (r.s.).
	5—8	Partners Set-and-honour.
A4	1—4	Circular-hey, with hands, two changes, to places, each man facing his partner (r.s.).
	5—8	Each man Set-and-honour with the contrary woman.

THE MERRY CONCEIT.

For four; in three parts (3rd Ed. 1665).

Music.		Movements.
		FIRST PART.
A	1—2	The two couples move forward a double and meet (r.s.).
	3—4	All turn single, men clockwise, women counter-clockwise.
	5—6	Couples fall back a double to places (r.s.).
	7—8	All turn single, women clockwise, men counter-clockwise.
B1	1—4	Each man four slips to his right in front of his partner, and four slips back to his place behind his partner, keeping his back to her.
	5—8	Each man arms the contrary woman with the right.
B2	1—4	Each man four slips to his right behind his partner, and four slips back to his place in front of his partner, keeping his face to her.
	5—8	Each man arms the contrary woman with the left.

THE MERRY CONCEIT—*continued.*

Music.		Movements.
		Second Part.
A	1—4	Each man turns his partner once round with his left hand, and then, taking the contrary woman by the right hand, changes places with her (r.s.).
	5—8	Each man, taking the contrary woman by the left hand, changes places with her, and then turns his partner once round with his right hand.
B1	1—8	First woman faces her partner, passes him by the right, turns to her right and, followed by her partner, walks between second man and second woman, turns to her left round second woman and returns to her place (w.s.).
B2	1—8	Second woman faces her partner and does the same.
		Third Part.
A	1—4	Each man back-to-back (Fig. 15, p. 17) with the contrary woman (r.s.).
	5—8	Each man back-to-back with his partner (r.s.).
B1	1—4	Each man turns out to his left and, followed by his partner, moves round three-quarters of a circle into the contrary woman's place (sk.s.).
	5—8	Partners Set-and-honour (Fig. 3, p. 11).
B2	1—4	Each woman turns out to her left and, followed by her partner, moves round to her own place (sk.s.).
	5—8	Each man Set-and-honour with the contrary woman.

ADSON'S SARABAND.

Longways for six; in three parts (1st Ed. 1650).

1	2	3
①	②	③

Music.		Movements
		First Part.
A1	1—4	All lead up a double and fall back a double to places (r.s.).
	5—8	Partners set and turn single.
A2	1—8	All that again.
B1	1—4	Men face left wall, move forward a double, turn round and return to places (r.s.).
	5—8	Men set to their partners and turn single.
B2	1—8	Women do the same to right wall.
		Second Part.
A1	1—2	Men face down and move forward a double obliquely to their left; while women face up and do the same (r.s.).
	3—4	Each file falls back a double, the men moving up into the women's places, and the women down into the men's (r.s.).
	5—8	Partners set and turn single.
A2	1—2	Men face up and move forward a double obliquely to their left; while women face down and do the same (r.s.).
	3—4	Same as in A1, the men moving down to places, the women up (r.s.).
	5—8	As in A1

ADSON'S SARABAND—*continued.*

Music.		Movements.
		SECOND PART—*contd.*
B1	Bar 1	First and second couples change places, first couple moving down between the second (sk.s.).
	Bar 2	First and third couples change places, third couple moving up between the first (sk.s.).
	3—4	Second and third couples change places, second couple moving down between the third (sk.s).
	5—8	Partners set and turn single.
B2	1—4	Same as in B1 to places, reversing the direction of the movements.
	5—8	Same as in B1.
		THIRD PART.
A1	1—4	Men face left wall, and both files move two doubles forward (r.s.).
	5—8	Partners face, set, and turn single.
A2	1—4	First and third men face each other, move forward a double on the outside of second man, meet, and fall back a double ; while first and third women do the same (r.s.).
	5—8	First and third men turn each other, while first and third women do the same. Simultaneously, second man turns his partner.
B1	1—4	Partners fall back two steps and change places (r.s.)
	5—8	Partners set and turn single.
B2	1—8	First man and first woman, followed by second and third couples, lead down the middle to the bottom, turn to their left and lead up to places (sk.s.).

CONFESS.

Longways for six; in four parts (1st Ed. 1650).

MUSIC		MOVEMENTS.
		FIRST PART.
A	1—4	The two files move forward a double, meet, and fall back a double to places (r.s.).
	5—8	That again.
B1	1—4	First man, standing between second and third women, leads them up a double, changes hands and leads them down a double; while second man in like manner leads first and fourth women down a double, changes hands and leads them up a double (r.s.).
	5—8	First man turns second man, second woman fourth woman, and third woman first woman.
B2	1—4	First man leads first and third women a double to left wall, changes hands, and leads them a double back to places; while second man does the same with the other women to right wall (r.s.).
	5—8	First man turns second man, first woman fourth woman, and third woman second woman.

CONFESS—*continued.*

Music.		Movements.
		SECOND PART.
A	1—8	First man, first woman and third woman face left wall; both files move forward two doubles, turn round and return to places (r.s.).
B1	1—2	First man and second woman fall back two steps, meet, and make an arch with right hands.
	3—8	The others hands-four round first man, passing under the arch (r.s.).
B2	1—2	Second man and first woman fall back two steps, meet, and make an arch with right hands.
	3—8	The others hands-four round second man, passing under the arch (r.s.).
		THIRD PART.
A	1—8	As in Second Part, to right wall.
B1	1—4	Second and third women lead up a double, change hands, and lead back to places; while first and fourth women lead down and do the same. Simultaneously, first man faces left wall, moves forward a double, turns round and moves back to his place; while second man does the same to right wall (r.s.).
	5—8	The women hands-four, while each man turns single twice.
B2	1—4	Same as in B1.
	5—8	The men turn each other, while each woman turns single twice.

CONFESS—*continued.*

Music.		Movements.
		FOURTH PART.
A	**1—8**	As in First Part.
B1	**1—4**	First man leads third woman down a double, changes hands and leads her up a double; while second man leads second woman down a double and does the same. Simultaneously, first and fourth women move up a double on the outside, turn round and return to places, passing under the arms of first man and third woman, and second man and second woman, respectively (r.s.).
	5—8	First woman turns fourth woman, first man third woman, and second man second woman.
B2	**1—4**	First man leads first woman up a double, changes hands and leads her down a double; while second man leads fourth woman up a double and does the same. Simultaneously, second and third women move down a double on the outside, turn round and return to places, passing under the arms of second man and fourth woman, and first man and first woman, respectively (r.s.).
	5—8	Second woman turns third woman, first man first woman, and second man fourth woman.

MAIDEN LANE.

Longways for six; in three parts (1st Ed. 1650).

	Music.	Movements.
		First Part.
A	1—4	All lead up a double and fall back a double to places (r.s.).
	5—8	That again.
B	1—4	All face left wall, move forward a double, and fall back to places (r.s.).
	5—8	Men the half-hey (Fig. 23, p. 26); while women do the same (sk.s.).
C	1—4	Partners set and turn single.
	5—8	That again.
		Second Part.
A	1—4	Partners side (r.s.).
	5–8	That again.
B	1—4	All fall back two small steps; partners cross over and change places (r.s.).
	5—8	All that again.
C	1—8	As in First Part.

MAIDEN LANE—*continued.*

Music.		Movements.
		THIRD PART.
A	1 — 4	Partners arm with the right.
	5—8	Partners arm with the left.
B	1 —2	First man changes places with second woman (r.s.).
	3— 4	First woman changes places with second man (r.s.); while third man changes places with his partner.
	5—6	First man changes places with third woman (r.s.).
	7—8	First woman changes places with third man; while second man changes places with his partner (r.s.).
C	1—8	As in First Part.

THE OLD MOLE.

Longways for six (1st Ed. 1650).

Music.		Movements.
A1	1—4	All lead up a double and fall back a double to places (r.s.).
	5—8	Partners set and turn single.
A2	1—8	All that again.
A3	1—4	All face left wall, move forward a double and fall back a double to places (r.s.).
	5—8	Partners set and turn single.
A4	1—4	All face right wall, move forward a double and fall back a double to places (r.s.).
	5—8	Partners set and turn single.
A5	1—4	First man and third woman meet and fall back to places (r.s.).
	5—8	First man and third woman change places (r.s.).
A6	1—8	First woman and third man the same.
A7	1—8	Second man and second woman the same.
A8	1—4	Second and third women take hands, move forward a double, and fall back a double to places ; while first and second men do the same (r.s.).

THE OLD MOLE—*continued.*

Music.		Movements.
	5—8	Second and third women, raising their arms, cross over to the women's side; while the third man passes under their arms and crosses to the men's side. Simultaneously, first and second men cross over to the men's side in like manner, the first woman passing under their arms (r.s.).
A9	1—8	Second and third men move forward and back and change places with the third woman, as in A8; while the first and second women do the same (r.s.).
A10	1—8	Same as A8.
A11	1—8	Same as A9.
A12	1—4	First man and third woman meet and fall back to places (r.s.).
	5—8	First man and third woman change places (r.s.).
A13	1—8	First woman and third man the same.
A14	1—8	Second man and second woman the same.
A15	1—2	Men take hands and move forward a double; while the women do the same (r.s.).
	3—4	First and third men and first and third women fall back a double to places (r.s).
	5—8	First man turns third man, and first woman turns third woman; while second man turns his partner.
A16	1—4	First man sides with third man, and first woman with third woman; while second man sides with his partner (r.s.).

THE OLD MOLE—*continued.*

Music.	Movements.
5—8	Each man turns his partner.
A17 1—8	Men the whole-hey (Fig. 23, p. 26), on their own side (sk.s.).
A18 1—8	Women the whole-hey on their own side (sk.s.).
A19 1—8	Circular-hey (Fig. 20, p. 21), first man and first woman passing by the right (sk.s.).
A20 1—8	That again.
A21 1—4	First man casts off to the lower end, followed by second and third men; while the women do the same (sk.s.).
5—8	First man casts off to the top, followed by second and third men ; while the women do the same (sk.s.).
A22 1—8	Same as in A2i.

SHEPHERD'S HOLIDAY.

Longways for six ; in three parts (1st **Ed.** 1650).

Music.		Movements.
		FIRST PART.
A1	1—4	All lead up a double and fall back a double to places (r.s.).
	5—6	Partners change places (r.s.).
A2	1—4	All lead down a double and fall back a double to places (r.s.)
	5—6	As in A1.
B1	1—2	First man and first woman slip in front of second man and second woman respectively.
	3—4	Third man and third woman slip behind second man and second woman respectively.
	5—8	First man, followed by second and third men, casts off to his left, and moves round in a circle to his place ; while first woman, followed by second and third women, casts off to her right and does the same (sk.s.).
B2	1—2	Third man and third woman slip in front of second man and second woman respectively.
	3—4	First man and first woman slip behind second man and second woman respectively.
	5—8	Third man, followed by second and first men, casts off to his right and moves round in a circle to his place ; while third woman, followed by second and first women, casts off to her left and does the same (sk.s.).

SHEPHERD'S HOLIDAY—*continued.*

Music.		Movements.
		SECOND PART.
A1	1—4	Partners side (r.s.).
	5—6	Partners change places (r.s.)
A2	1—6	All that again to places.
B1	1—4	The men take hands, fall back a double, and move forward a double to places; while the women do the same (r.s.).
	5—8	Men hands-threee; while women do the same.
B2	1—4	Same as in B1.
	5—8	Men hands-three, facing outward; while women do the same.
		THIRD PART.
A1	1—4	Partners arm with the right.
	5—6	Partners change places (r.s.).
A2	1—4	Partners arm with the left.
	5—6	Partners change places (r.s.).
B1	1—2	First man changes places with second woman (r.s.).
	3—4	Second man changes places with first woman (r.s.).
	5—8	Third man and third woman cross over and cast up to first woman's and first man's places (sk.s.).
B2	1—2	Third woman changes places with second man (r.s.).
	3—4	Second woman changes places with third man (r.s.).
	5—8	First woman and first man cross over and cast up to places (sk.s.).

UPON A SUMMER'S DAY.

Longways for six; in three parts (1st Ed. 1650).

MUSIC.		MOVEMENTS.
		FIRST PART.
A1	1—4	All lead up a double and fall back a double to places (r.s.).
	5—8	Partners set and turn single.
A2	1—8	All that again.
B1	1—4	Men take hands, move forward a double and fall back a double to places; while women take hands and do the same (r.s.).
	5—8	Second and third men keep hands joined and make an arch; while second and third women do the same. First man casts off, passes under the arms of second and third men and moves to the lowest place; while first woman does the same on her own side (sk.s.).
B2	1—4	As in B1.
	5—8	As in B1, second couple moving down to lowest place.
B3	1—4	As in B1.
	5—8	As in B1, to places.

UPON A SUMMER'S DAY—*continued.*

Music.		Movements.
		SECOND PART.
A1	1—4	Partners side (r.s.).
	5—8	Partners set and turn single.
A2	1—8	All that again.
B1, B2 & B3		As in First Part.
		THIRD PART.
A1	1—4	Partners arm with the right.
	5—8	Partners set and turn single.
A2	1—4	Partners arm with the left.
	5—8	Partners set and turn single.
B1, B2 & B3		As in First Part.

BROOM, THE BONNY, BONNY BROOM.

Longways for eight; in three parts (1st Ed. 1650).

Music.		Movements.
		First Part.
A1	1—4	All lead up a double and fall back a double to places (r.s.).
	5—8	First man, followed by second man, casts off and returns to his place; while first woman, followed by second woman, fourth man followed by third man, and fourth woman followed by third woman, do the same (r.s.).
A2	1—4	All lead down a double and fall back a double to places (r.s.).
	5—8	As in A1.
A3	1—4	Second man and second woman fall back; whilst first and third couples move forward a double, meet, and fall back a double (r.s.).
	5—8	First and third couples hands-four.
A4	1—4	Third man and third woman fall back; while second and fourth couples move forward a double, meet, and fall back a double (r.s.).
	5—8	Second and fourth couples hands-four.

BROOM, THE BONNY, BONNY BROOM—*continued.*

Music.		Movements.
		SECOND PART.
A1	1—4	Partners side (r.s.).
	5—8	Partners set and turn single.
A2	1—8	All that again.
A3	1—2	First and second men take both hands and change places; while first and second women do the same.
	3—4	Third and fourth men take both hands and change places: while third and fourth women do the same.
	5—8	Partners set and turn single.
A4	1—4	As in A3 to places.
	5—8	Partners set and turn single.
		THIRD PART.
A1	1—4	Partners arm with the right.
	5—8	Partners set and turn single.
A2	1—4	Partners arm with the left.
	5—8	Partners set and turn single.
A3	1—4	The two middle men lead to the left wall, change hands and lead back again; while the two middle women do the same to the right wall. Simultaneously, first man and first woman lead up, change hands and lead back again; while fourth man and fourth woman lead down, change hands and lead back again (r.s.).
	5—8	Hands-eight, half-way round.
A4	1—8	Same movement as in A3 to places.

LADY SPELLOR.

Longways for eight ; in three parts (1st Ed. 1650).

| 1 | 2 | 3 | 4 |

| ① | ② | ③ | ④ |

Music.		Movements.

FIRST PART.

A1	1—4	All lead up a double and fall back a double to places (r.s.).
	5—8	Partners set and turn single.
A2	1—8	All that again.
A3	1—4	Men face left wall and all move forward two doubles (r.s.).
	5—8	Men face their partners. Partners set and turn single.
A4	1—4	Partners fall back two steps and change places (r.s.).
	5—8	Partners set and turn single.
A5	1—8	First man and first woman, followed by second, third and fourth couples, lead down the middle to the bottom, turn to their left, and lead up to places (sk.s.).

SECOND PART.

A1	1—4	Partners side (r.s.).
	5—8	Partners set and turn single.
A2	1—8	All that again.
A3, A4, & A5		As in First Part.

THIRD PART.

A1	1—4	Partners arm with the right.
	5—8	Partners set and turn single.
A2	1—4	Partners arm with the left.
	5—8	Partners set and turn single.
A3, A4, & A5		As in First Part.

LORD OF CARNARVON'S JIG.

Longways for eight; in four parts (1st Ed. 1650).

Music.		Movements.
		FIRST PART.
A1	1—4	All lead up a double and fall back a double to places (r.s.).
	5—8	That again.
B1	1—4	Each couple whole-gip, facing outward (Fig. 17, p. 19) (r.s.).
	5—8	That again, counter-clockwise.
A2	1 – 4	First man and first woman cross over, pass behind second woman and second man, respectively, and fall into the second place, the second couple moving up one place (sk.s.)
	5 –8	First man and first woman cross over, pass behind third man and third woman, respectively, and fall into the third place, the third couple moving up one place (sk.s.).
B2	1—4	First man and first woman lead down between fourth man and fourth woman and cast off to the top, the man to his right, followed by fourth, third and second men, the woman to her left, followed by fourth, third and second women (sk.s.).
	5—8	Partners arm with the right.

LORD OF CARNARVON'S JIG—*continued.*

Music.		Movements.
		SECOND PART.
A1	1—4	All lead down a double and fall back a double to places (r.s.).
	5—8	That again.
B1	1—8	As in B1, First Part.
A2	1—4	Second man and second woman cross over, pass behind third woman and third man, respectively, and fall into the third place, the third couple moving down one place (sk.s).
	5—8	Second man and second woman cross over, pass behind fourth man and fourth woman, respectively, and fall into the second place, the fourth couple moving down one place (sk.s.).
B2	1—4	Second man and second woman lead up between first man and first woman, and cast off to the bottom, the man to his left, followed by first, fourth and third men, the woman to her right, followed by first, fourth and third women (sk.s.).
	5—8	Partners arm with the left.
		THIRD PART.
A1	1—8	As in First Part.
B1	1—8	As in First Part.
A2	1—8	As in First Part, the third man and the third woman crossing over, successively, into the second and third place.

LORD OF CARNARVON'S JIG—*continued*.

Music.		Movements.
		THIRD PART—*contd.*
B2	1—4	As in First Part, the third man and the third woman leading to the bottom and casting off to the top, the man followed by second, first and fourth men, the woman followed by second, first and fourth women.
	5—8	Partners arm with the right.
		FOURTH PART.
A1	1—8	As in Second Part.
B1	1—8	As in First Part.
A2	1—8	As in Second Part, the fourth man and fourth woman crossing over, successively, into the third and second place.
B2	1—4	As in Second Part, the fourth man and fourth woman leading up to the top and casting off to the bottom, the man followed by third, second and first men, the woman by third, second and first women.
	5—8	Partners arm with the left.

LULL ME BEYOND THEE.

Longways for eight; in three parts (1st Ed. 1650).

[3]	[1]	(2)	(4)
(3)	(1)	[2]	[4]

MUSIC.		MOVEMENTS.
		FIRST PART.
A	1—4	All move forward a double, meet, and fall back a double to places (r.s.).
	5—8	That again.
B1	1—2	First man and second woman lead out to the left wall, and second man and first woman to right wall; while third and fourth couples move down and up, respectively, and meet (r.s.).
	3—4	First and third couples, four abreast, take hands, and fall back a double toward the Presence; while second and fourth couples, facing the Presence, take hands and fall back a double (r.s.).
	5—8	All move forward, and each man turns the woman opposite to him.
B2	1—2	Third couple leads up a double, and fourth couple leads down a double; while first man and second woman and second man and first woman move forward a double and meet (r.s.).
	3—4	First and third men, second and fourth women, four abreast, take hands and fall back a double toward left wall; while the other four take hands and fall back a double toward right wall (r.s.).
	5—8	All move forward and each man turns his partner.

LULL ME BEYOND THEE—*continued.*

Music.		Movements.
		SECOND PART.
A	1—4	Partners side (r.s.).
	5—8	Third and fourth men side with their partners; while first man sides with second woman, and second man with first woman (r.s.).
B1	1—4	First and third men, and second and fourth women take hands, move forward a double to left wall, and fall back a double to places; while the other four do the same to the right wall (r.s.).
	5—8	First and third men, and second and fourth women, hands-four to places; while the other four do the same.
B2	1—4	First and third couples, four abreast (first man on the left, first woman on the right), lead up a double and fall back a double; while second and fourth couples lead down a double and fall back a double (r.s.).
	5—8	First and third couples hands-four to places; while second and fourth couples do the same.
		THIRD PART.
A	1—4	Partners arm with the right (r.s.).
	5—8	Third and fourth men arm their partners with the left; while first man arms with second woman, and second man with first woman in like manner.

LULL ME BEYOND THEE—*continued*.

Music.	Movements.
	THIRD PART—*contd.*
B1 1—2	First man and second woman lead out a double to left wall, and second man and first woman to right wall ; while third and fourth couples move forward and meet (r.s.). Third man and fourth woman then take hands and face left wall; while fourth man and third woman take hands and face right wall.
3—4	First man and second woman, and second man and first woman, lead back to places, holding up their hands. Simultaneously, third man and fourth woman lead out to left wall, passing under the arch made by first man and second woman ; while fourth man and third woman, passing under the arch made by second man and first woman, do likewise (r.s.).
5—8	Each man turns the woman he is handing.
B2 1—2	First couple leads up a double, and second couple down a double ; while third man and fourth woman, fourth man and third woman, move forward and meet (r.s.). Third man and third woman take hands and face up ; while fourth man and fourth woman take hands and face down.

LULL ME BEYOND THEE—*continued.*

MUSIC.	MOVEMENTS.
	THIRD PART—*contd.*
3—4	First and second couples lead back to places, holding up their hands. Simultaneously, third man and third woman lead up to places, passing under the arch made by first man and first woman; while fourth man and fourth woman, passing under the arch made by second man and second woman, lead down and do likewise (r.s.).
5—8	Each man turns his partner.

NOTATION.   **83**

THE MERRY, MERRY MILKMAIDS.

Longways for eight; in three parts (1st Ed. 1650).

```
 ┌─┐     ┌─┐     ┌─┐     ┌─┐
 │1│     │2│     │3│     │4│
 └─┘     └─┘     └─┘     └─┘

 (1)     (2)     (3)     (4)
```

Music.		Movements.
		FIRST PART.
A1	1—4	All lead up a double and fall back a double to places (r.s.).
	5—8	Partners set and turn single.
A2	1—8	All that again.
B1	1—2	First man and first woman meet; while third man and third woman do the same (r.s.).
	3—4	First and second couples change places, first couple slipping down between second man and second woman; while third and fourth couples change places in like manner.
	5—8	All fall back a double and move forward a double to places (r.s.).
	9—12	First and second couples right-hands-across; while third and fourth couples do the same.
B2	1—2	Second man and second woman meet; while fourth man and fourth woman do the same (r.s.).
	3—4	First and second couples change places, second couple slipping down between first man and first woman; while third and fourth couples change places in like manner.
	5—12	Same as in B1.

THE MERRY, MERRY MILKMAIDS—*continued.*

Music.		Movements.
		SECOND PART.
A1	1—4	Partners side (r.s.).
	5—8	Partners set and turn single.
A2	1—8	All that again.
B1	1—4	First man, followed by second, third and fourth men, turns out to his left, and casts down to the lower end (sk.s.).
	5—8	First woman, followed by second, third and fourth women, turns out to her right, and casts down to lower end (sk.s.).
	9—12	Partners set and turn single.
B2	1—4	First man turns out to his right and, followed by the rest of the men, casts up to the top (sk.s.).
	5—8	First woman turns out to her left and, followed by the rest of the women, casts up to the top (sk.s.).
	9—12	Partners set and turn single.
		THIRD PART.
A1	1—4	Partners arm with the right.
	5—8	Partners set and turn single.
A2	1—4	Partners arm with the left.
	5—8	Partners set and turn single.
B1	1—4	Men fall back a double and move forward a double to places (r.s.).
	5—12	Men the Whole-hey (Fig. 22, p. 24), first and second men facing each other, third and fourth men the same (sk.s.).
B2	1—12	Women do the same as the men.

THE PHŒNIX.

Longways for eight (4th Ed. 1670).

| 1 | 2 | 3 | 4 |

| ① | ② | ③ | ④ |

Music,		Movements.
A1	1—4	All lead up a double and fall back a double to places (r.s.).
	5—8	That again.
B1	1—4	Partners set and turn single.
	5—8	That again.
A2	1—4	First man crosses over and, followed by the other men, casts down outside the women and stands behind the fourth woman (sk.s.). Women turn and face the men.
	5—8	Each man takes the woman in front of him by both hands, puts her back a double and pulls her forward a double to her place (r.s.).
B2	1—4	All fall back two steps ; each man changes places with the woman opposite him (r.s.).
	5—8	All that again.
A3	1—8	Women do as the men did in A2.
B3	1—8	Same as in B2.
A4	1—4	Fourth man and fourth woman cross over, and, followed by the third couple (not crossing), second couple (crossing), and first couple (not crossing), move down the middle to bottom place (sk.s.). All take hands in a ring.

THE PHŒNIX—*continued.*

Music.		Movements.
	5—8	Hands-eight, once round.
B4	1—4	Partners set and turn single.
	5—8	That again.
A5	1—4	Each man turns the woman on his right.
	5—8	Men hands-four.
B5	1—4	First and fourth women move forward a double meet, and fall back a double co places, turning single as they do so; while second and third women do the same (r.s.).
	5—8	Men do the same.
A6	1—4	Each man turns his partner.
	5—8	Women hands-four.
B6	1—8	Same as in B5, the men doing it first.
A7	1—8	Each file the Whole-hey (Fig. 22, p. 24), first man facing second woman, third man fourth woman, second man first woman, and fourth man third woman (sk.s.).
B7	1—4	Partners set and turn single.
	5—8	That again.
A8	1—4	Fourth man and fourth woman cross over, and, followed by third couple (not crossing), second couple (crossing), and first couple (not crossing), move up the middle to the top place (sk.s.).
	5—8	Fourth man turns out to his left and, followed by the other men, casts down to his original place; while fourth woman turns out to her right and, followed by the other women, does the same (sk.s.).
B8	1—4	Partners set and turn single.
	5—8	That again.

SPRING GARDEN.

Longways for eight; in three parts (3rd Ed. 1665).

Music.	Movements.
	FIRST PART.
A 1—4	All lead up a double and fall back a double to places (r.s.).
5—8	That again.
B1 Bar 1	All fall back two steps.
2—4	The two upper couples hands-four half-way round; while the two lower couples do the same.
5—6	The two files fall back two steps and move forward two steps.
7—8	Partners at the top and bottom change places. Simultaneously, the two middle men change places; while the two middle women do the same (r.s.).
B2, B3, & B4	Same as in B1. All are now in their original places.
	SECOND PART.
A 1—2	First and second men move backward, each into the other's place; while third and fourth men, first and second women, and third and fourth women do the same (r.s.).
3—4	Partners change places (r.s.).
5—8	All that again to places.

SPRING GARDEN—*continued.*

Music.		Movements.
		SECOND PART—*contd.*
B1	1—4	First man, followed by second man, casts off and moves down into the second place, second man falling on the outside of first man, and both facing down; while fourth man, followed by third man, casts off and moves up into the third place, third man falling on the outside, and both facing up (r.s.). Simultaneously, first and fourth women, followed by second and third women, respectively, cast off and do likewise.
	5—8	Second and third men, first and fourth men, first and fourth women, and second and third women set and change places (r.s.).
B2	1—4	The two files face. Third man turns out to his right and casts off into the fourth man's place, the fourth man following him and falling immediately above him on his left; while third woman turns out to her left and casts off into the fourth woman's place, the fourth woman following her and falling immediately above her on her right. Simultaneously, second man and second woman, followed by first man and first woman, respectively, cast off and do likewise (r.s.).
	5—8	Partners set and change places (r.s.).
B3	1—4	Same movement as in B1, the fourth man and fourth woman casting off and moving down into the second place, the first man and first woman casting off and moving up into the third place.

SPRING GARDEN—*continued.*

Music.	Movements.
	SECOND PART—*contd.*
5—8	Same as in B1.
B4 1—4	Same movement as in B2. Couples are now in their proper order, the men on the women's side, and the women on the men's.
5—8	Partners set and change places (r.s.).
	THIRD PART.
A 1—2	All face left wall and move forward a double (r.s.).
3—4	Partners face and change places (r.s.).
5—6	All face right wall and move forward a double (r.s.)
7—8	Partners face and change places (r.s.).
B1 1—2	All fall back two steps and move forward two steps to places (r.s.).
3—4	First and fourth couples face each other and move forward a double ; while second couple slips up into the first place, and third couple slips down into the bottom place.
5—8	Partners at the top and bottom arm with the right ; while the two middle men and the two middle women do likewise.
B2 1—8	Same movement as in B1, the second and third couples meeting in the middle, and all arming with the left. All are now in their original places.
B3 1—8	Same as in B1.
B4 1—8	Same as in B2.

BOBBING JOE.

Longways for as many as will; in six parts (1st Ed. 1650).

Music.		Movements.
		FIRST PART.
A	1—4	All lead up a double and fall back a double to places (r.s.).
	5—8	That again.
B	1—4	Partners set and turn single.
	5—8	That again.
		SECOND PART. (Duple minor-set.)
A	1—2	First man and first woman slip down between second man and second woman, the second couple slipping up into the first place.
	3—4	Second man and second woman slip down between first man and first woman, the first couple slipping up into the first place.
	5—8	First and second couples hands-four.
B	Bar 1	First man snaps his fingers at second man on the second beat of the bar.
	Bar 2	Second man snaps his fingers at first man on the second beat of the bar.
	3—4	First and second men change places (r.s.).
	Bar 5	First woman snaps her fingers at second woman on the second beat of the bar.
	Bar 6	Second woman snaps her fingers at first woman on the second beat of the bar.
	7—8	First and second women change places (r.s.) (progressive).

BOBBING JOE—*continued.*

Music.		Movements.
		THIRD PART.
A	1—4	Partners side (r.s.).
	5—8	That again.
B	1—4	Partners set and turn single.
	5—8	That again.

		FOURTH PART.
		(Duple minor-set.)
A	1—4	First and second men take hands, fall back a double, and move forward a double to places ; while first and second women do the same (r.s.).
	5—8	First man turns outward to his left and, followed by second man, casts off and returns to his place ; while first woman turns outward to her right and, followed by second woman, does the same (r.s.).
B	Bar 1	First and second men snap their fingers at their partners on the second beat of the bar.
	Bar 2	First and second women do the same.
	3—4	Partners cross and change places (r.s.).
	5—8	First and second couples hands-four, half-way round (progressive).

		FIFTH PART.
A	1—4	Partners arm with the right.
	5—8	Partners arm with the left.
B	1—4	Partners set and turn single.
	5—8	That again.

BOBBING JOE—*continued.*

Music.		Movements.
		Sixth Part.
		(Duple minor-set.)
A	1—4	First and second men fall back a double, and move forward a double to places (r.s.).
	5—8	First and second women do the same.
B	Bar 1	First man snaps his fingers at second man on the second beat of the bar; while first woman does the same at second woman.
	Bar 2	Second man snaps his fingers at first man on the second beat of the bar; while second woman does the same at first woman.
	3—4	First and second men change places; while first and second women do the same (r.s.).
	Bar 5	First man snaps his fingers at first woman on the second beat of the bar; while second man does the same at second woman.
	Bar 6	First woman snaps her fingers at first man on the second beat of the bar; while second woman does the same at second man.
	7—8	Partners change places (r.s.) (progressive: improper).*

* In the succeeding rounds those on the men's side do as the first two men did in the first round, and those on the women's side as the first two women did.

CATCHING OF FLEAS.

Longways for as many as will; in three parts (4th Ed. 1670).

Music.		Movements.
		FIRST PART.
A	1—4	All lead up a double and fall back a double to places (r.s.).
	5—8	That again.
B (repeated ad lib.)		(Duple minor-set.)
	1—4	First man and first woman fall back two steps, move forward, take right hands and change places (r.s.).
	5—8	First man and first woman slip down into second place, cross over and change places (r.s.); while second couple moves up into first place (progressive).

CATCHING OF FLEAS—*continued.*

Music.	Movements.
	Second Part.
A 1—4	Partners side (r.s.).
5—8	That again.
B (repeated ad lib.)	(Duple minor-set.)
1—2	First man crosses over into second woman's place, and first woman into second man's place (sk.s.); while second couple moves up into first place.
3—4	First man and first woman change places (progressive).
5 - 8	Second man turns out to his left and, followed by first man, casts off and returns to the same place; while second woman turns out to her right and, followed by first woman, does the same (sk.s.).
	Third Part.
A 1—4	Partners arm with the right.
5—8	Partners arm with the left.
B (repeated ad lib.)	(Duple minor-set.)
1—4	First man and first woman cast off into second place and return up the middle to places (sk.s.).
5—8	First man and first woman take hands, slip down into second place, release hands, and turn single; while second couple moves up into first place (progressive).

THE FRIAR AND THE NUN.

Longways for as many as will; in three parts (1st. Ed. 1650).

Music.		Movements.
		FIRST PART.
A	1—4	Men move up a double (r.s.), and turn single.
	5—8	Women do the same.
	9—12	Women fall back a double to places (r.s.), and turn single.
	13—16	Men do the same.
		SECOND PART.
		(Duple minor-set.)
A	1—4	First and second men fall back a double (r.s.), and turn single.
	5—8	First and second women do the same.
	9—12	Partners change places (r.s.).
	13—14	First and second men change places; while first and second women do the same (r.s.).
	15 – 16	Partners change places (r.s.) (progressive).

Country Dance Book. Part III.   G

THE FRIAR AND THE NUN—*continued.*

Music.	Movements.
	Third Part.
	(Duple minor-set.)
A　1—4	First and second men turn each other once-and-a-half round, change places, and face each other ; while first and second women do the same.
5—6	All slip inwards, first man and second woman to their right, second man and first woman to their left.
7—8	All four turn single.
9—10	First and second couples hands-four, half-way round.
11—12	All four turn single.
13—14	First and second couples right-hands-across, half-way round (progressive).
15—16	All four turn single.

THE IRISH LADY, OR ANISEED WATER ROBIN.

Longways for as many as will; in four parts (1st Ed. 1650).

| 1 | 2 | 3 | 4 | • • • • • |
| ① | ② | ③ | ④ | • • • • • |

Music.		Movements.
		FIRST PART.
A	1—4	All lead up a double and fall back a double to places (r.s.).
	5—8	That again.
B	1—4	Partners set and turn single.
	5—8	That again.
		SECOND PART.
		(Duple minor-set.)
A	1—4	First man and second woman Whole-gip, (Fig. 16, p. 18) once-and-a-half round, facing centre, falling into each other's places.
	5—8	First woman and second man do the same.
B	1—2	First man and second woman change places (r.s.).
	3—4	Second man and first woman do the same.
	5—8	First couple casts off into the second place, second couple moving up (sk.s.) (progressive).

THE IRISH LADY, OR ANISEED WATER ROBIN—
continued.

Music.		Movements.
		THIRD PART.
		(Duple minor-set.)
A	1—8	First man crosses over below second woman, turns round her to his left, crosses again above second man, passes round him, and returns to his place. Simultaneously, first woman crosses over above second man (passing first man by the left), turns to her left, passes round second man, crosses over above second woman, turns to her right, round second woman, and returns up the middle to her place (sk.s.)
B	1—4	First and second couples right-hands-across (sk.s.).
	5—8	As in Second Part (progressive).
		FOURTH PART.
		(Duple minor-set.)
A	1—2	First man and second man take right hands and change places; while first and second women take left hands and do the same (r.s.).
	3—6	First man moves up on the outside of second man; while first woman moves up on the outside of second woman. All take hands and, four abreast, lead up a double and fall back a double (r.s.).
	7—8	First man, followed by second man, casts off to his left, and returns up the middle to his place : while first woman, followed by second woman, casts off to her right and does the same (sk.s.).
B	1—2	Partners change places (r.s.).
	3—4	First man changes places with second woman (r.s.).
	5—6	Second man changes places with first woman (progressive).
	7—8	All turn single.

IRISH TROT.

Longways for as many as will; in three parts (1st Ed. 1650).

Music.		Movements.
		FIRST PART.
A1	1—4	All lead up a double and fall back a double to places (r.s.).
	5—8	Partners set and turn single.
A2	1—4	All lead down a double and fall back a double to places (r.s.).
	5—8	As in A1.
		SECOND PART.
		(Duple minor-set.)
A1	Bar 1	First man and first woman take right hands, then left hands.
	Bar 2	First man and first woman hold their hands crossed and change places, slipping round clockwise.
	3—4	Both fall back four small steps (r.s.).
	5—8	First man and first woman meet, and arm with the right.
A2	1—2	First man and second woman change places in like manner; while first woman and second man do the same (progressive; improper).
	3—4	First man and second woman take hands and fall back four small steps; while first woman and second man do the same (r.s.).
	5—8	Partners arm with the right.

If partners on reaching the bottom of the dance are on their wrong sides, they must change over while they are neutral.

IRISH TROT—*continued.*

Music.		Movements.

THIRD PART.

A1 1—4 All lead up a double and fall back a double to places (r.s.).

5—8 First man, followed by the other men, turns out to his left, and casts down to the bottom; while first woman, followed by the other women, turns out to her right and does likewise (sk.s.).

A2 1—8 First man and first woman take left hands, turn out to their left and, followed by the other couples, cast up to the top, turn again to their left, and return down the middle to the bottom place (sk.s.).

A3 1—4 All lead down a double and fall back a double to places (r.s.).

5—8 First man, followed by the other men, turns out to his right, and casts up to the top; while first woman, followed by the other women, turns out to her left and does likewise (sk.s.).

A4 1—8 First man and first woman take right hands, turn out to their right and, followed by the other couples, cast down to the bottom, turn again to their right, and return up the middle to places (sk.s.).

———

Playford gives another Part, which has been omitted in the text.

THE NEW FIGARY.

Longways for as many as will (4th Ed. 1670).

Music.		Movements.
		(Duple minor-set.)
A	1—4	All lead up a double and fall back a double to places (r.s.).
	5—8	That again.
B	1—4	First man honours second woman and turns her.
	5—8	Second man does the same to first woman.
C	1—4	First man and second woman back-to-back (Fig. 15, p. 17) (r.s.).
	5—8	Second man and first woman the same.
D	Bar 1	First and second men clap hands on the first beat of the bar, and strike their right hands together on the middle beat; while first and second women do the same.
	Bar 2	Same again, striking left hands together.
	3—4	All four turn single.
	Bar 5	First man and first woman clap hands on the first beat of the bar, and strike their right hands together on the middle beat; while second man and second woman do the same.
	Bar 6	That again, striking left hands together.
	7—8	First man and first woman cast off into the second place; while second couple moves up into the first place (progressive).

At the beginning of the second and succeeding rounds all the couples lead up, as at the first; or, if preferred, this movement may, from the beginning of the dance, be confined to those couples only who are actively engaged in the progressive movement.

ROW WELL, YE MARINERS.

Longways for as many as will; in two parts (1st Ed. 1650).

| 1 | 2 | 3 | 4 | . | . | . | . | . |

| ① | ② | ③ | ④ | . | . | . | . | . |

MUSIC.		MOVEMENTS.
		FIRST PART.
Λ	1—4	All lead up a double and fall back a double to places (r.s.).
	5—8	That again.
B	Bar 1	First man faces up and moves two slips to his left.
	Bar 2	First woman faces up and moves two slips to her right.
	Bar 3	First man slips back to his place.
	Bar 4	First woman slips back to her place.
C	1—4	First man and first woman face each other, fall back a double, and move forward a double to places (r.s.).
D	Bar 1	First man and first woman clap hands on the first beat of the bar, and strike their right hands together on the middle beat.
	Bar 2	Same again, striking left hands together.
	Bar 3	First man claps hands on the first beat of the bar, and strikes his chest with both hands on the middle beat; while the first woman does the same.
	Bar 4	First man and first woman strike both their hands together (right on left and left on right) on the first beat of the bar.
	5—8	All that again, striking left hands first.

ROW WELL YE MARINERS—*continued.*

Music.		Movements.
		SECOND PART.
		(Duple minor-set.)
A	1—4	First and second men side; while first and second women do the same (r.s.).
	5—8	First and second men honour and change places; while first and second women do the same (progressive).
B	1—4	As in First Part, first and second men doing as the first man did, first and second women as the first woman did.
C	1—4	All four fall back a double and move forward a double to places (r.s.).
D	1—8	Both couples do as first man and first woman did in First Part.

It will probably be found more effective to omit the First Part altogether.

SWEET KATE.

Longways for as many as will; in three parts (4th Ed. 1670).

Music.		Movements.
		First Part.
A	1—4	All lead up a double and fall back a double to places (r.s.).
	5—8	That again.
B1	Bar 1	On the first beat of the bar all spring on to left feet; on the middle beat, partners strike right feet together, swinging them sideways from right to left.
	Bar 2	That again, springing on to right feet, and striking left feet together.
	Bar 3	On the first beat of the bar all clap hands; on the middle beat partners strike right hands together.
	Bar 4	That again, partners striking left hands together.
	Bar 5	During the first half of the bar all turn their hands as though they were winding wool; on the middle beat each one holds up one finger of the right hand,
	Bar 6	That again, holding up left hands.
	7—8	All turn single.
B2	1—8	Same as in B1.

SWEET KATE—*continued.*

Music.	Movements.
	SECOND PART.
A 1—4	Partners side (r.s.).
5—8	That again.
B1 & B2	Same as in First Part.
	THIRD PART.
A 1—4	Partners arm with the right.
5—8	Partners arm with the left.
B1 & B2	Same as in First Part.

TOUCH AND TAKE.

Longways for as many as will (2nd Ed. 1652).

Music.		Movements.
A1	1—4	All lead up a double and fall back a double to places (r.s.).
	5—8	Partners set and turn single.
A2	1—8	All that again.
		(Duple Minor-Set.)
A3	1—2	First man and first woman cross over and stand, the man behind the second woman, and the woman behind the second man (r.s.).
	3—4	First man, placing his hands on the shoulders of second woman, turns her half-way round, so that she faces him; while first woman does the same to second man.
	5—8	All four set and turn single, moving up into the first place.
A4	1—4	First man and second woman lead down a double and fall back a double; while first woman and second man do the same (r.s.).
	5—8	All four set and turn single, staying in the first place.

TOUCH AND TAKE—*continued.*

Music.		Movements.
A5	1—2	First man turns second woman half-way round to her original position, and passes on to the third woman ; while first woman does the same to second man, and passes on to the third man (progressive).
	3—8	Same as in A3.
A6	1—8	Same as in A4.

The rest of the dance is done in the usual way, except that partners, upon reaching the bottom of the Set, change places while they are neutral. Partners, upon reaching the top of the Set, remain neutral for one round (16 bars), and then cross over as first man and first woman did in A3.

All, therefore, will go down the dance on the wrong side, and come up on the proper side.

THE

COUNTRY DANCE BOOK

PART IV.

CONTAINING

FORTY-THREE COUNTRY DANCES

FROM

THE ENGLISH DANCING MASTER

(1650—1728)

DESCRIBED BY

CECIL J. SHARP

AND

GEORGE BUTTERWORTH.

LONDON: NOVELLO AND COMPANY, LIMITED.
NEW YORK: THE H. W. GRAY CO., SOLE AGENTS FOR THE U.S.A.

CONTENTS.

———

LONGWAYS FOR AS MANY AS WILL.

THE DANCE.

THE ROOM.

THE following diagram is a ground plan of the room in which the dances are supposed to take place :—

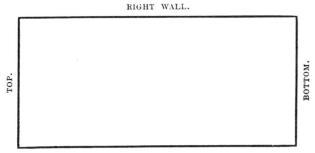

RIGHT WALL.

TOP.

BOTTOM.

LEFT WALL.

A diagram, showing the initial disposition of the dancers, is printed at the head of the notation of each dance, and placed so that its four sides correspond with the four sides of the room as depicted in the above plan. That is, the upper and lower sides of the diagram represent, respectively, the right and left walls of the room ; its left and right sides the top and bottom.

In Playford's time, the top of the room was called *the Presence*, alluding to the dais upon which the spectators were seated. The expression *facing the Presence* means, therefore, facing up, *i.e.*, toward the top of the room ; while *back to the Presence* means facing down, toward the bottom of the room.

TECHNICAL TERMS AND SYMBOLS.

In the following pages, certain symbols and technical expressions are used. These will now be defined.

O = man ; ☐ = woman.

r. = a step taken with the right foot ; l. = a step taken with the left foot.

h.r. = a hop off the right foot ; l.r. = a hop off the left foot.

f.t. = feet-together.

∩ a spring.

A *Longways dance* is one in which the performers take partners and stand in two parallel lines, those on the *men's side* facing the right wall, those on the *women's side* facing the left wall.

The *General Set* denotes the above formation, *i.e.*, the area enclosed by the dancers.

A *Progressive movement*, or *figure*, is one which leaves the dancers relatively in different positions.

A *Progressive dance* consists of the repetition, for an indefinite number of times, of a series of movements one of which is progressive, the execution of each repetition resulting, therefore, in a change of position of some, or all of the performers. Each performance of one complete series of movements is called a *Round*.

There are two types of progression called, respectively, *Whole-set* and *Minor-set*.

In a *Whole-set* dance the progression is effected by the transference of the top couple to the bottom of the General Set, each of the remaining couples moving up one place. The *Minor-set* dance is one in which the figures contained in each round are performed simultaneously by subsidiary groups of two (*duple*), or three (*triple*). adjacent couples.

A *neutral* dancer is one who is passive during the performance of a round. Normally, in a Minor-set dance, each couple, on reaching either end of the General Set, remains neutral during the next round, and sometimes the following one as well.*

The disposition of the dancers in a longways dance is said to be *proper* when men and women are on their own sides; and *improper* when the men are on the women's side and the women on the men's.

In dances, or figures, in which two couples only are engaged, the terms *contrary woman* and *contrary man* are used to denote the woman or man other than the partner.

When two dancers, standing side by side, are directed to *take hands* they are to join inside hands : that is, the right hand of one with the left hand of the other, if the two face the same way ; and right hands or left hands, if they face in opposite directions. When they are directed to take, or give, right or left hands, they are to join right with right, or left with left.

To *cross hands* the man takes the right and left hands of the woman with, respectively, his right and left hands, the right hands being held above the left.

When two dancers face one another and are directed to take *both hands,* they are to join right with left and left with right.

To pass *by the right* is to pass right shoulder to right shoulder ; *by the left,* left shoulder to left shoulder.

When two dancers pass each other they should always, unless otherwise directed, pass each other by the right.

When a woman's path crosses that of a man's, the man should allow the woman to pass first and in front of him.

---

* For further and more detailed information on this point see *The Country Dance Book,* Part I., pp. 18—24.

When one dancer is told to *lead* another, the two join right or left hands according as the second dancer stands on the right or left hand of the leader.

To *cast off* is to turn outward and dance outside the General Set.

To *cast up* or *cast down* is to turn outward and move up or down outside the General Set.

To *fall* hither or thither is to dance backwards; to *lead*, or *move*, is to dance forwards.

To make a *half-turn* is to turn through half a circle and face in the opposite direction; to make a *whole-turn* is to make a complete revolution.

The terms *clockwise* and *counter-clockwise* are self-explanatory and refer to the direction of circular movements.

THE MUSIC.

The several strains of each dance-air will be marked in the music-book and in the notation by means of capital letters, A, B, C, etc.   When a strain is played more than once in a Part it will be marked A1, B1, C1, etc., on its first performance, and A2, B2, C2, A3, B3, etc., in subsequent repetitions.

It will be found that most of the dances in this collection are divided into two or more Parts.   John Essex quaintly but aptly likened these divisions to " the several verses of songs upon the same tune ".

In non-progressive dances, the division is made merely for the sake of clearness in description; the Parts are intended to follow on without pause.

When, however, a progressive movement occurs in one or other of the figures of a Part, that Part must be repeated as often as the dancers decree.   The usual practice is to repeat the Part until the leader has returned to his original place at the top of the General Set.

Progressive figures will be marked as such in the notation ; while the Parts in which they occur will be headed " Whole-Set ", " Duple Minor-Set ", etc., according to the nature of the progression.

THE STEPS.

Country Dance steps always fall on the main beats of the bar, whether the time be simple or compound. When the step itself is a compound one, that is, when it consists of more than one movement, the accented movement always falls upon the beginning of the beat.

RUNNING-STEP.

A bounding or slow running step, executed upon the ball of the foot with a moderate amount of spring, forward rather than upward, and with limbs relaxed. The arms, held loosely, should be slightly bent at the elbow and allowed to swing naturally and rhythmically.

In the notation this step will be called :—

r.s. (running-step).

WALKING-STEP.

This is a springy walking step executed, at any rate by the men, with a nonchalant bearing and a certain jauntiness of manner not easily described. Technically, the fundamental distinction between the ordinary walking-step and that used in the country dance is that in the former the weight of the body is gradually transferred from one foot to the other (both feet, at one moment of the movement, being on the ground at the same time), and each step is taken first on the heel and then on the ball of the foot ; whereas, in the country-dance walking-step, the movement from one foot to the other is effected by means of a very small spring and is executed entirely on the ball of the foot. In other words, the step is in reality a modified form of the running-step, in which the spring, though present, is scarcely noticeable.

In the notation this will be called :—

w.s. (walking-step).

SKIPPING-STEP.

This is a step and hop first on one foot and then on the other. The hop is made forward rather than up, and should raise the body as little as possible. When the steps are long and the motion rapid, the hop should be scarcely perceptible.

The accent is on the step, which must fall, therefore, on the beginning of the beat. The hop falls on the last quarter, or the last third of the beat, according as the latter is simple or compound, thus :—

In the notation this step will be called :—

sk.s. (skipping-step).

THE SLIP.

This, like the preceding, is a compound step. It is used in moving sideways along the straight, or around a circle, the dancer facing at right angles to the line of motion.

The performer stands with feet apart. If moving, say, to the left, a low spring is made off the left foot and the weight of the body transferred to the right foot, which alights close to the spot just vacated by the left foot. The left foot then falls to the ground, twelve inches or more to the side, a spring is again made off it, with a side thrust imparted by the right foot, and the movements are repeated. The legs are thus alternately opening and closing, scissors-fashion.

The accent falls on the foot off which the spring is made, that is, the left or right, according as the motion is toward the left or right. thus : —

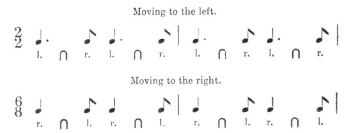

The slip is used, though not invariably, in ring movements and whenever the dancers are directed to move sideways, or " slip " to right or left.

THE DOUBLE-HOP.

This is sometimes used in ring movements, as an alternative to the preceding step. It is a variant of the Slip, in which the feet, instead of taking the ground one after the other, alight together, about six inches apart. The movement is, therefore, a series of jumps or double-hops.

THE SINGLE.

This consists of two movements. A step forward, or to the side, is made with one foot, say, the right, and the weight of the body supported upon it. The left foot is then drawn up and the heel placed in the hollow of the right foot (one bar).

As the left foot is moved up to the right, the body is raised
upon the instep of the right foot, and lowered as the feet
come together.   These movements are shown in the following
diagram :—

The double is three steps, forward or backward, followed by
" feet-together," thus :—

THE FIGURES.

FIGURE 1.

TURN SINGLE.

The   dancer   moves   round   in   a   small   circle,   clockwise
(unless otherwise directed), taking four small running-steps,[*]
beginning with the right foot.   When the turn is directed to
be made counter-clockwise, the first step is taken with the
left foot.

Care must be taken to keep the body erect, but not stiff,
and to time the turn so that the dancer reaches his original
position exactly on the conclusion of the last step.

FIGURE 2.

THE SET.

This is a formal movement of courtesy, addressed by one
dancer to another or, more frequently, by two dancers to each

---

* In dances in triple time the movement is completed in three steps.

other, simultaneously. It consists of a single to the right, followed by a single to the left (two bars), thus :—

FIGURE 3.

THE SET-AND-HONOUR.

In certain dances four instead of two bars are allotted to the Set. This may be simply an abbreviation, or misprint, for Set-and-turn-single; or it may bear a literal interpretation, in which case it is, perhaps, advisable to interpolate the Honour (Fig. 11, p. 16) after each single, thus : —

Whenever set-and-honour occurs in the text, performers may either execute it in the way just described, or substitute the set-and-turn-single.

FIGURE 4.

THE SIDE.

This, like the set, is a movement of courtesy, performed by two dancers, usually partners, but not necessarily so.

The two dancers face each other and then move forward a double (w.s. or r.s.) obliquely to the right, passing by the left, and on the last step (f.t.) making a half-turn counter-clockwise and so facing each other (two bars). This completes the first half of the movement and is called *side to the right*. In the second half of the movement—*side to the left*—the dancers retrace their steps along the same tracks and return to their original places, beginning with the left foot, moving obliquely to the left, passing by the right, and turning clockwise on the "feet-together" to face each other, thus :—

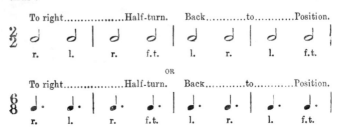

The dancers must remember to face each other at the beginning of each movement, to pass close to each other shoulder to shoulder, and always to face in the direction in which they are moving.

Figure 5.

ARM WITH THE RIGHT.

Two performers, usually partners, meet, link right arms, swing round a complete circle clockwise, separate and fall back to places (r.s.) (four bars). The precise moment at which the dancers unlink depends upon circumstances, but it is usually on the fifth or sixth step.

Figure 6.

ARM WITH THE LEFT.

This is similar to the preceding movement, the dancers linking left instead of right arms, and swinging round counter-clockwise instead of clockwise.

FIGURE 7.

ALL LEAD UP A DOUBLE AND FALL BACK A DOUBLE TO PLACES.

Couples stand in column formation, facing up. Each man then leads his partner up a double and, without turning or releasing hands, falls back a double (four bars).

FIGURE 8.

ALL LEAD UP A DOUBLE, CHANGE HANDS AND LEAD BACK

A DOUBLE.

All lead up a double as in the preceding figure. They then release and change hands, make a half-turn toward each other, face downwards, and lead a double back to places (four bars).

FIGURE 9.

HANDS-THREE, HANDS-FOUR, ETC.

Three or more dancers, as directed, extend and join hands, dance round in a ring clockwise, facing centre, make one complete circuit, separate, and return to places.

If more or less than one circuit is to be made, specific instructions to that effect will be given in the notation, *e.g.*, half-way round, once-and-a-half round, etc. In the absence of any such directions it is to be understood that one complete circuit is to be danced.

The performers should clasp hands firmly, lean outward, and not dance too daintily. When the movement is followed by a repetition in the reverse direction, the dancers, without releasing hands, may stamp on the first beat of the second movement.

Occasionally, this figure is performed facing outward, that is, with backs toward the centre. Whenever this occurs special instructions to that effect will be given in the notation.

FIGURE 10.

THE TURN.

Two dancers face each other, join both hands, swing round clockwise, separate, and return to places.

In swinging, performers should clasp hands firmly, and lean outward as in the ring movement. If either the skipping- or the running-step be used the feet should be slightly crossed so that the dancers may face each other throughout the movement.

FIGURE 11.

THE HONOUR.

This, like the Set, is a formal movement of courtesy addressed by one dancer to another, or by two dancers to each other simultaneously.

In making the honour, the woman curtseys, and the man bows and, if he is wearing one, raises his hat.

The old custom was for partners to honour each other at the beginning and at the close of each dance—the latter should never be omitted. The movement should always be done in rhythm with the music.

Figure 12.

HALF-POUSSETTE.

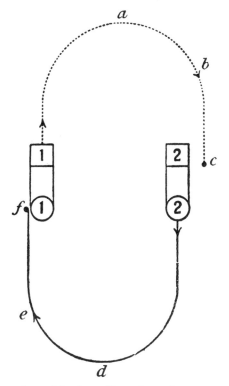

This is performed by two adjacent couples.

Each man faces his partner and takes her by both hands. The arms must be held out straight, and very nearly shoulder high.

First man, pushing his partner before him, moves four steps along dotted line to *a*, and then falls back four steps along the line *a b c* into the second couple's place, pulling his partner after him.

Simultaneously, second man, pulling his partner with him, falls back four steps along unbroken line to *d*, and then moves forward four steps along the line *d e f* into the first couple's place (four bars).

The above movement is called the half-poussette, and is, of course, a progressive figure.

When the half-poussette is followed by a repetition of the same movement, each couple describing a complete circle or ellipse, the figure is called the whole-poussette.

FIGURE 13.

BACK-TO-BACK.

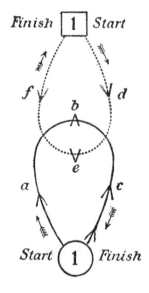

First man and first woman face each other and move forward, the man along the line *a b*, the woman along the dotted line *d e*. They pass by the right, move round each other, back to back, and fall back to places, the man along the line *b c*, the woman along the dotted line *e f*.

The arrow heads in the diagram show the positions of the dancers at the end of each bar and point in the directions in which they are facing. The arrows outside the lines show the direction in which the dancers move.

FIGURE 14.

WHOLE-GIP FACING CENTRE.

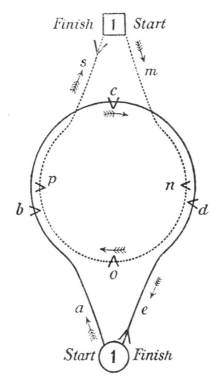

First man moves forward along line *a*, dances round circle *b c d*, keeping his face toward the centre, and falls back along line *d e* to place; while first woman dances along dotted line *m*, moves round circle *n o p*, keeping her face toward the centre, and falls back along dotted line *p s* to place (four bars).

The arrows and arrow heads have the same signification as in the preceding figure.

FIGURE 15.

WHOLE-GIP FACING OUTWARD.

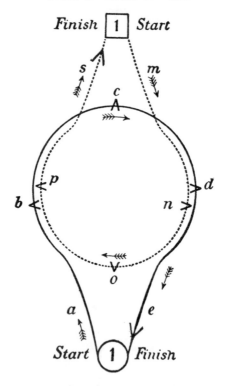

First man moves along line *a* and dances round circle *b c d*, facing outward, to place; while first woman moves along dotted line *m*, dances round circle *n o p*, facing outward, and moves along dotted line *p s* to place (four bars).

Figure 16.

RIGHT-HANDS-ACROSS.

This is performed usually by four dancers (say, first and second couples), but occasionally by three.

In the former case, first man and second woman join right hands, while second man and first woman do the same. Holding their hands close together, chin-high, the four dancers dance round clockwise to places, all facing in the direction in which they are moving.

When three performers only are dancing, two of them clasp right hands while the third places his right hand on the hands of the others.

Figure 17.

LEFT-HANDS-ACROSS.

This is very similar to the preceding figure, the dancers joining left instead of right hands and dancing round counter-clockwise instead of clockwise.

It is to be understood that in both of these figures the dancers make one complete circuit unless specific instructions to the contrary are given.

THE HEY.

The Hey may be defined as the rhythmical interlacing in serpentine fashion of two groups of dancers, moving in single file and in opposite directions.

The figure assumes different forms according to the disposition of the dancers. These varieties, however, fall naturally into two main types according as the track described by the dancers—disregarding the deviations made by them in passing one another—is (1) a straight line, or (2) the perimeter of a closed figure, circle or ellipse.

The second of these species, as the simpler of the two, will be first explained.

FIGURE 18.

THE CIRCULAR HEY.

In the analysis that follows the circle will, for the sake of convenience, be used throughout to represent the track described by the dancers in this form of the figure. In the round dance the track will, of course, be a true circle; while in the square dance it will become one as soon as the movement has begun. On the other hand, in a longways dance, the formation will be elliptical, rather than circular, but this will not affect the validity of the following explanation.

In the circular-hey the dancers, who must be even in number, are stationed, at equal distances, around the circumference of a circle, facing alternately in opposite directions, thus :—

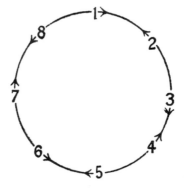

DIAGRAM A.

Odd numbers face and move round clockwise; even numbers counter-clockwise. All move at the same rate and, upon meeting, pass alternately by the right and left.

This progression is shown in diagram B, the dotted and unbroken lines indicating the tracks described, respectively, by odd and even numbers. It will be seen that in every circuit the two opposing groups of dancers, odd and even, thread through each other twice; that is, there will be eight simultaneous passings, or *changes*, as we will call them, in each complete circuit :—

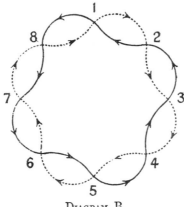

DIAGRAM B.

This movement is identical with that of the Grand Chain, except that in the familiar Lancers' figure the performers take hands, alternately right and left, as they pass; whereas, in the Country Dance hey, "handing," as Playford calls it, is the exception rather than the rule.

In this form the hey presents no difficulty. No misconception can arise so long as (1) the initial dispositions of the pairs, and (2) the duration of the movement, measured by circuits or changes, are clearly defined. And instructions on these two points will always be given in the notation. It should be understood that, in the absence of directions to the contrary, (1) the first pass is by the right, and (2) the dancers pass without handing.

FIGURE 19.

PROGRESSIVE CIRCULAR HEY.

Sometimes the hey is danced progressively, the dancers beginning and ending the movement pair by pair, instead of

simultaneously, as above described.   This is effected in the
following way :—

The first change is performed by one pair only, say Nos. 1
and 2 (see diagram A, Fig. 18); the second by two pairs,
Nos. 1 and 3, and Nos. 2 and 8; the third, in like manner, by
three pairs ; and the fourth by four pairs.   At the conclusion
of the fourth change Nos. 1 and 2 will be face to face, each
having traversed half a circuit, and all the dancers will be
actively engaged, thus :—

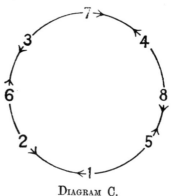

DIAGRAM C.

The movement now proceeds in the usual way.   At the
end of every complete circuit the position will be as follows :—

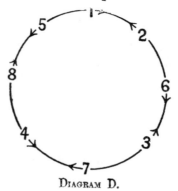

DIAGRAM D.

The figure is concluded in the following manner :—
Nos. 1 and 2, upon reaching their original places (see
diagram D), stop and remain neutral for the rest of the
movement. The others continue dancing until they reach
their proper places when they, in like manner, stop and
become neutral. This they will do, pair by pair, in the
following order, Nos. 3 and 8, 4 and 7, 5 and 6. The initial
and final movements thus occupy the same time, *i.e.*, four
changes.

Whenever the progressive hey occurs (1) the initial pair
will be named ; and (2) the duration of the movement,
measured by changes or circuits, will be given in the notation.

Figure 20.

THE STRAIGHT HEY.

The dancers stand in a straight line at equi-distant stations,
alternately facing up and down, thus :—

Top → 1 2 → 3 ← 4 → 5 ← 6 → 7 ← 8 ← *Bottom*

Diagram E.

Odd numbers face down ; even numbers up. As in the
circular hey the dancers move at an even rate, and pass each
other alternately by the right and left. The movement is
shown in diagram F, the dotted and unbroken lines indicating,
respectively, the upward and downward tracks described by
the dancers :—

Top 1 *a* 2 3 4 5 6 7 *a* 8 *Bottom*
b   *c*

Diagram F.

From this diagram it will be seen that the movements of
individual dancers are the same as those of the couples in a

progressive Country Dance (duple minor-set), with this difference—that the neutrals, instead of remaining passive, reverse their direction by moving round the loops *d c* or *b a*.

In the first change, all the dancers will be actively engaged, meeting and passing each other, and there will be no neutrals. But in the second change, there will be two neutrals, Nos. 2 and 7, both of whom will turn to their right and move, No. 2 round the loop *b a*, No. 7 round the loop *d c*. In the third change, Nos. 2 and 7, having reversed their directions, re-enter the track and all the dancers pass, in pairs, as in the first change. In this way the track is converted into an endless path and the continuous and characteristic rhythmic movement of the hey is preserved.

When, therefore, the number of dancers is even, as in the above example, there will be, in alternate rounds, (1) no neutrals, and (2) two neutrals, one at each end.

The distribution, however, will be somewhat different when the number of dancers is uneven, as the following diagram will show :—

DIAGRAM G.

Odd numbers face down ; even numbers up. No.5,being neutral in the first change, will turn out to his left and move along the dotted line *a* preparatory to passing No. 3 by the left in the next change. In the second change, No. 2, being neutral at the upper end, will turn to his right and move round the loop *d c* and reverse his direction.

When this variation is performed by three dancers only, we have the form in which the hey occurs very frequently in the Country Dance. For this reason it will perhaps be advisable to describe this particular form in detail.

FIGURE 21.

THE HEY FOR THREE.

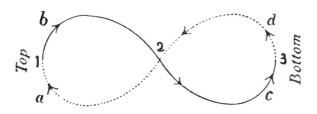

The movement is executed in six changes in the following way :—

(1.) Nos. 1 and 2 face each other and pass by the right, No. 1 moving along the unbroken line, No. 2 along the dotted line ; while No. 3 faces up and gets ready to pass No. 1 by the left in the next change—and this he may do in two different ways, presently to be described.

(2.) Nos. 1 and 3 pass by the left, No. 1 moving along the unbroken line, No. 3 along the dotted line ; while No. 2 reverses his direction by bearing to his right and moving round the top loop from *a* to *b*.

(3.) Nos. 2 and 3 pass by the right, No. 2 moving along the unbroken line, No. 3 along the dotted line ; while No. 1 bears to his left, moves round the bottom loop from *c* to *d* and reverses his direction.

This completes the first half of the figure, called the *half-hey*. Nos. 1 and 3 have changed ends, while No. 2 is in his original station.

(4.) Nos. 1 and 2 pass by the left, No. 1 moving along the dotted line, No. 2 along the unbroken line ; while No. 3 bears to his right, moves round the top loop from *a* to *b* and reverses his direction.

(5.) Nos. 1 and 3 pass by the right, No. 1 along the dotted line, No. 3 along the unbroken line ; while No. 2 bears to his left, moves round the bottom loop from *c* to *d* and reverses his direction.

(6.) Nos. 2 and 3 pass by the left to places ; while No. 1 bears to his right and moves into his place.

This completes the figure— the *whole-hey*—and the dancers are once again in their original positions.

The nature of the preparatory movement made by No. 3 during the first change depends upon the initial disposition of the three dancers. If, for instance, the position is that of a longways dance for six, and all the dancers are facing front, No. 3's initial movement will depend upon the file to which he belongs. If on the men's side, he will merely move forward in a curve toward the middle of the General Set in preparation for the left-pass in the second change. If on the women's side, she will turn out to her left and cast up, bearing a little to her right, *i.e.*, outward and away from the General Set.

The above is presumably the correct way in which the hey-for-three should be executed in the Country Dance, although we have no direct evidence that it was in fact so danced in Playford's day. Hogarth, however, in his *Analysis of Beauty* (1753), after defining the hey as " a cypher of S's, a number of serpentine lines interlacing and intervolving one another," prints a diagram of the hey-for-three which, although it might have been clearer, seems to show that the way the figure was danced at that period was substantially the same as that described above.

Moreover, Wilson (*The Analysis of Country Dancing*, 1811) also describes the figure and prints a diagram, of which the following—except that for clearness' sake the tracks are differentiated by means of varied lines—is a faithful reproduction :—

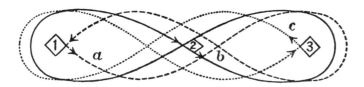

No. 1 moves along the broken line *a* ; No. 2 along the line *b* ; and No. 3 along the dotted line *c*.

Except that the two half-heys are inverted—the two *lower* dancers beginning the movement and passing by the *left*— the method shown in the diagram is precisely the same as that we have above described.

The straight-hey may be performed progressively. It is unnecessary, however, to describe in detail the way in which this is effected, because, in principle, the method is the same as that already explained in Fig. 19.

Playford makes frequent use of the expressions " Single Hey " and "Double Hey." It is difficult to say with certainty what he means by these terms, because he uses them very loosely. Very often they are identical with what we have called the straight- and circular-hey. As, however, this is not always the case, I have, with some reluctance, substituted the terms used in the text, which are self-explanatory and free from ambiguity.

GENERAL INSTRUCTIONS.

The preceding explanations of the steps, figures, etc., will, it is hoped, enable the reader to comprehend and to interpret the Notations which are now to follow. It should be remembered, however, that, although every movement be executed with scientific precision, this is but the first step toward the goal which every dancer should have in view. Technical proficiency, of itself, is of little worth. To the performer who is infected with the true spirit of the dance, technique is merely the vehicle of artistic expression.

Now the dominant characteristic of the English Country Dance is its " gay simplicity "—gaiety expressed by simple, easy, unaffected movements. Pointing the toe, arching the leg, affecting a swaying and mincing gait, all movements, indeed, devised to achieve a conventional elegance, are alien to the true spirit of this dance. Such devices are the stock-in-trade of the self-conscious dancer, ever mindful of his own appearance and the impression which he is making upon the onlookers. They are not the movements of those whose sole aim is self-expression, who dance for the joy of dancing and the rich opportunity it offers for the exercise of those emotional and imaginative faculties, for which, in the ordinary rough-and-tumble of everyday life, it is not easy to find an outlet. Affected movements are not bad only because they are ugly—though that may be reason enough— but primarily because they are self-conscious, self-consciousness being, of course, the arch-foe of all natural instinctive, artistic expression.

Now, the English Country-Dance, prior at any rate to the 18th century, had never throughout its recorded history been used as a spectacle for the entertainment of others. It had always been danced for its own sake ; for the purpose of self-expression, not self-glorification ; as an art, not a pageant. And therein, of course, lies its unique value.

The technique of the Country-Dance is really a very simple one. The steps are all easy and natural, while the execution of the figures, even the most elaborate, presents but little difficulty when once the dancer has grasped the conception that motion is not so much a matter of the legs as of body-balance —a principle to which every traditional folk-dancer instinctively conforms. If the beginner will only seize this principle, leave his feet to take care of themselves,—remembering that they are supports, not ornaments,—always incline his body according to the direction of his motion, and concentrate his attention wholly upon the figures, he will soon acquire all the technique required of the Country Dancer.

Again, performers must never forget the intimate relationship which should always exist between the dance and the tune to which it is set. After all, the movements of the dance are but the interpretation or translation, in terms of bodily action, of the music upon which they are woven—just as the melody of a song is primarily the musical expression of the words to which it is wedded. For this reason, the dancer should carefully listen to the tune to which he is about to dance, assimilate it thoroughly and, if possible, commit it to memory. In particular, let him take careful note of its construction, *i.e.*, the number, character, and relative lengths of its several strains, in order that he may time and " phrase " his movements in accordance with them. The *tempo* of the dance should be determined by the character of its tune, that is, solely upon musical considerations. The application of this principle, viz., the subordination of the dance to the music, is absolutely imperative in the present case. For the Playford dances are very persistent in type, and, were it not for the wide range of the emotional content of the tunes, it would be extremely difficult to give to them the requisite variety of treatment.

Although style in the matter of art is intuitive rather than to be acquired by precept, a question of feeling, not of thought, and is altogether too subtle, elusive and intangible a thing to be captured and set down in words, the following maxims may, nevertheless, be of some help to the beginner, the more particularly if they be taken as suggestions rather than rules :—

(1.) Make no movement, however insignificant, that is not rhythmically in agreement with the music. For instance, in giving or taking a hand in the hey, or when " leading ", begin the movement in plenty of time—two or more beats before-hand—and take care to raise and move the arm in rhythm with the music.

(2.) When " leading ", do not regard the taking of hands as a mere formality. The leader should actually lead—that is, guide and regulate the movements of his partner.

(3.) The Country-Dance is a concerted or group-dance. A large part of the enjoyment derived from country-dancing arises directly from the cultivation by the dancers of a communal feeling and understanding. This has, of course, its technical counterpart in the harmonizing of the movements of each individual with those of the other dancers—an art in itself, and one only acquired after much practice and experience.

(4.) Before beginning a figure from rest, make some preliminary rhythmical movement (akin to the " Once-to-yourself ", or the preparatory jump made before each figure of the Morris Dance), so that you may start easily and naturally with the music. The purpose of "the two steps back ", the initial movement of so many figures, is to give the dancer a rhythmical balance preparatory to the execution of the movement.

(5.) Remember that the dances in the Notations are divided into Parts, figures, etc., merely for the purpose of clear description. The aim of the dancer should be to conceal, not to call attention to these divisions; rather, perhaps, to regard the successive figures of a dance as the subordinate parts of a complete sentence, giving to each no more than its due emphasis.

(6.) The steps prescribed in the Notation are not obligatory. Nor is uniformity necessary, *i.e.*, that every dancer should use the same step at the same time; nor, again, that a single figure should always be danced to one step throughout —the arbitrary change of step in the course of a movement is not only permissible, but is in many cases to be commended.

(7.) In taking a step, be careful not to glide, *i.e.*, gradually to transfer the weight of the body from one foot to the other. Crawling is not dancing. The spring, however slight it may be—and it should always be as low as possible— is an essential element of every Country-Dance step.

NOTATION.

PUT ON THY SMOCK ON A MONDAY.
Round for six; in three parts (4th Ed. 1670).

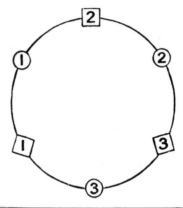

MUSIC.		MOVEMENTS.
		FIRST PART.
A1	1—4	Hands-six, eight slips clockwise.
	5—8	Partners set and turn single.
A2	1—4	Hands-six, eight slips counter-clockwise to places.
	5—8	Partners set and turn single.
A3	1—4	First man leads first and second women forward a double towards third woman, and falls back a double (r.s.).
	5—8	First man turns third woman; while first and second women turn each other.
A4	1—8	As in A3, first man leading third and first women forward towards second woman, first man turning second woman, first and third women turning each other.

PUT ON THY SMOCK ON A MONDAY—*continued.*

MUSIC.		MOVEMENTS.
		First Part—*continued.*
A5	1—8	As in A3, first man leading second and third women forward towards first woman, first man turning his partner, second and third women turning each other.
		Second Part.
A1	1—4	Sides all.
	5—8	Partners set and turn single.
A2	1—8	All that again.
A3, A4 and **A5**		As in First Part, second man doing as first man did.
		Third Part.
A1	1—4	Partners arm with the right.
	5—8	Partners set and turn single.
A2	1—4	Partners arm with the left.
	5—8	Partners set and turn single.
A3, A4 and **A5**		As in First Part, third man doing as first man did.

THE GELDING OF THE DEVIL.

Round for six ; in three parts (3rd Ed., 1665).

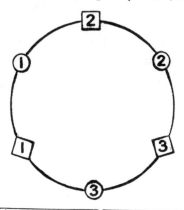

MUSIC.		MOVEMENTS.
		FIRST PART.
A	1—8	Hands-six, eight slips clockwise and eight slips counter-clockwise to places.
B1	1—4	First man and first woman lead forward a double and fall back a double to places (r.s.).
	5—8	Leading forward again (r.s.), they pass between second man and third woman and cast off (sk.s.) to places, the first man to his left outside second couple, and the first woman to her right outside third couple.
B2	1—8	As in B1, second couple leading forward and passing between first woman and third man.
B3	1—8	As in B1, third couple leading forward and passing between first man and second woman.

THE GELDING OF THE DEVIL—*continued.*

MUSIC.		MOVEMENTS.
		SECOND PART.
A	1—4	Sides all.
	5—8	That again.
B1, B2 and **B3.**		As in First Part.
		THIRD PART.
A	1—4	Partners arm with the right.
	5—8	Partners arm with the left.
B1, B2 and **B3**		As in First Part.

OAKEN LEAVES.

Round for eight ; in three parts (4th Ed., 1670).

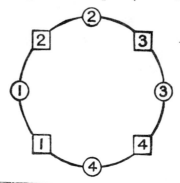

MUSIC.		MOVEMENTS.
		FIRST PART.
A1	1—4	Hands-all, eight slips clockwise.
	5—8	Partners set and turn single.
A2	1—4	Hands-all, eight slips counter-clockwise to places.
	5—8	Partners set and turn single.
A3	1—2	First and second men change places (r.s.).
	3—4	First and second women change places (r.s.).
	5—8	First and second couples circular-hey to places, two changes, partners facing.
A4	1—8	Third and fourth couples do likewise.
		N.B.—*This Part can, if desired, be made equal in length to each of the subsequent Parts, if the movements in A3 and A4 be repeated, respectively, by the first and fourth couples and by the second and third couples.*

OAKEN LEAVES—*continued.*

MUSIC.		MOVEMENTS.
		SECOND PART.
A1	1—4	Partners side.
	5—8	Partners set and turn single.
A2	1—8	All that again.
A3	1—4	Men lead out their partners a double, away from the centre, change hands, and lead them back again.
	5—	Men, passing in front of their partners, turn the next woman on their right once round.
A4, A5 and **A6**		Movement in A3 repeated three times to places, the men in each repetition leading out the women they have just turned.
		THIRD PART.
A1	1— 4	Partners arm with the right.
	5—8	Partners set and turn single.
A2	1—4	Partners arm with the left.
	5—8	Partners set and turn single.
A3	1—4	The men move forward a double to the centre and fall back a double to places.
	5—8	Each man turns the woman on his left once-and-a-half round, and moves into her partner's place.
A4, A5, and **A6.**		Movement in A3 repeated three times to places, the men in each repetition turning the women on their left and passing on, clockwise, into the next man's place.

SELLENGER'S ROUND; OR, THE BEGINNING OF THE WORLD.

Round for as many as will ; in four parts (4th Ed. 1670).

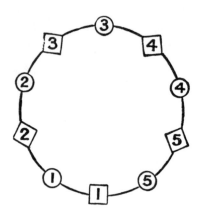

MUSIC.		MOVEMENTS.
		FIRST PART.
A.	1—8	Hands-all, eight slips clockwise and eight slips counter-clockwise to places.
B1	1—2	All move forward two singles toward the centre, beginning the first with the right foot, and the second with the left.
	3—4	All fall back a double to places.
	5—8	Partners set and turn single.
B2	1—8	All that again.

SELLENGER'S ROUND—*continued.*

MUSIC.		MOVEMENTS.
		SECOND PART.
A.	1—4	All take hands, move forward a double to the centre, and fall back a double to places.
	5—8	That again.
B1 and **B2**		As in First Part.
		THIRD PART.
A.	1—4	Partners side.
	5—8	That again.
B1 and **B2**		As in First Part.
		FOURTH PART.
A.	1—4	Partners arm with the right.
	5--8	Partners arm with the left.
B1 and **B2**		As in First Part.

HEARTSEASE.

For four ; in three parts (1st Ed. 1650).

MUSIC.		MOVEMENTS.
		Running-step throughout the dance.
		FIRST PART.
A	1—4	Couples move forward a double, meet, and fall back a double to places.
	5—8	That again.
B1	1—4	First man and second woman face down ; first woman and second man face up. All fall back a double and move forward a double.
	5—8	First man and second woman turn with right hands and fall back to places ; while second man and first woman do the same.
B2	1 4	All fall back a double and move forward a double to places.
	5—8	Partners turn with left hands.
		SECOND PART.
A	1—4	Partners side.
	5—8	Contraries side.
B1 and **B2**		As in First Part.
		THIRD PART.
A	1—4	Partners arm with the right.
	5—8	Contraries arm with the left.
B1 and **B2**		As in First Part.

HIT AND MISS.

For four ; in three parts (1st Ed. 1650).

MUSIC.		MOVEMENTS.
		Running-step throughout the dance.
		FIRST PART.
A	1—4	Couples move forward a **double, meet, and** fall back a double to places.
	5—8	That again.
B	1—2	Couples move forward a double and meet.
	3—4	First man leads second woman up a double, while second man leads first woman down a double.
	5—6	Both couples turn and face one another. First man leads second woman down a double ; while second man leads first woman up a double.
	7—8	First man and first woman, joining right hands, fall back a double to places ; while second man and second woman do the same.
C	1—6	Circular-hey, partners facing, four changes.
		SECOND PART.
A	1—4	Sides all.
	5—8	That again.
B and C		As in First Part.
		THIRD PART.
A	1—4	Partners arm with the right.
	5—8	Partners arm with the left.
B and C		As in First Part.

THE BOATMAN.

Longways for six; in three parts (1st Ed. 1650).

MUSIC.		MOVEMENTS.
		Running-step throughout the dance.
		FIRST PART.
A1	1—4	All lead up a double and fall back a double to places.
	5—8	Partners set and turn single.
A2	1—8	All that again.
B1	1—4	First couple and second man the straight-hey, four changes (the three standing in line, second man in the middle facing first woman and passing her by the right); while the third couple and second woman do the same (the latter facing third man and passing him by the right).
	5—8	Partners turn, the first and third couples once round, the second couple half-way round. *All are now in their opposite places.*
B2	1—4	As in B1, except that second man heys with third couple (facing third woman and passing her by the right) while second woman heys with first couple) (facing first man and passing him by the right).
	5—8	Partners turn as in B1, to places.

THE BOATMAN—*continued.*

MUSIC.		MOVEMENTS.
		SECOND PART.
A1	1—4	Sides all.
	5—8	Partners set and turn single.
A2	1—8	All that again.
B1	1—2	First couple and second man hands-three half-way round and stand in line facing down, second man in the middle ; while third couple and second woman do likewise and stand in line facing up, second woman in the middle.
	3—4	Still holding hands, all fall back two steps and move forward two steps.
	5—8	Second man and second woman meet in the middle of the Set, turn each other once-and-a-quarter round and fall into the middle station (improper) ; while first and third men turn their partners once round. *All are now in their opposite places.*
B2	1—2	As in B1, except that second man hands-three half-way round with third couple, second woman with first couple.
	3—8	As in B1, to places.

THE BOATMAN—*continued*.

MUSIC.		MOVEMENTS.
		THIRD PART.
A1	1— 4	Partners arm with the right.
	5—8	Partners set and turn single.
A2	1—4	Partners arm with the left.
	5—8	Partners set and turn single.
B1	1—4	First and third men and second woman hands-three round second man to places.
	5—8	Second man turns his partner.
B2	1— 4	First and third women and second man hands-three round second woman to places.
	5—8	Second man turns his partner.

THE WHIRLIGIG.

Longways for six; in three parts (1st Ed. 1650).

$$\boxed{1} \qquad \boxed{2} \qquad \boxed{3}$$

$$\textcircled{1} \qquad \textcircled{2} \qquad \textcircled{3}$$

MUSIC.		MOVEMENTS.
		FIRST PART.
A1	1—4	All lead up a double and fall back a double to places.
	5—8	That again.
B1	1—4	Second man and second woman lead up the middle to the top, cast off and return to places.
	5—8	Second woman crosses over, passes counter-clockwise round first man and returns to her place; while second man crosses over, passes clockwise round first woman and returns to his place (r.s.).
B2	1—4	Second man and second woman lead dowr the middle to the bottom, cast off and return to places.
	5—8	Second woman crosses over, passes clockwise round third man and returns to her place; while second man crosses over, passes counter-clockwise round third woman and returns to his place (r.s.).
A2	1—4	First man, followed by second and third men, casts off to the bottom; while first woman, followed by second and third women, does the same (sk.s.).

THE WHIRLIGIG—*continued.*

MUSIC.		MOVEMENTS.
		FIRST PART—*continued.*
	5—8	Second man and second woman, followed respectively by third man and third woman, lead down the middle, pass between first man and first woman, and cast off to the top, the men to their right, the women to their left (progressive) (sk.s.).
		The movements in B1, B2 and A2 are now repeated twice to places as in a progressive longways dance (Whole-set), the third couple occupying the middle position in the first repetition, and the first couple in the last.
		SECOND PART.
A1	1—4	Partners side.
	5—8	That again.
B1	1—8	Second man crosses over, arms first woman with the right, and then goes the whole-hey with the first couple, second man facing first man and passing him by the *left*. Simultaneously, second woman arms third man with the right and goes the whole-hey with the third couple, second woman facing third woman and passing her by the *left* (r.s.).
B2	1—8	As in B1 to places, second man arming third man with the right and heying with the third couple; second woman arming first woman and heying with the first couple.
A2	1—8	As in First Part (progressive).
		The movements in B1, B2 and A2 are now repeated twice progressively to places.

THE WHIRLIGIG—*continued.*

MUSIC.		MOVEMENTS.
		THIRD PART.
A1	1—4	Partners arm with the right.
	5—8	Partners arm with the left.
B1	1—4	First man, followed by second man, casts down into the second place, and returns up the middle to his own place ; while first woman, followed by second woman, does the same (r.s.).
	5—8	First and second couples right-hands-across (r.s.).
B2	1—4	Third man and third woman, followed respectively by second man and second woman, cast up and return down the middle to places.
	5—8	Second and third couples right-hands-across.
A2	1—8	As in First Part (progressive).
		The movements in B1, B2 and A2 are now repeated twice progressively to places.

PICKING UP STICKS.

Longways for six ; in three parts (1st Ed. 1650).

| 1 | 2 | 3 |

| ① | ② | ③ |

MUSIC.		MOVEMENTS.
		FIRST PART.
A1	1—4	All lead up a double and fall back a double to places.
	5—8	That again.
A2	1—4	First man changes places with the middle dancer on the opposite side and then with the last dancer on his own side (r.s.).
	5—8	All lead up a double and fall back a double to places.
A3	1—4	First woman does as first man did in **A2**.
	5—8	As in **A2**.
A4	1—4	Second woman does as first man did in **A2**.
	5—8	As in **A2**.
A5	1—4	Second man does as first man did in **A2**.
	5—8	As in **A2**.
A6	1—4	Third man does as first man did in **A2**.
	5—8	As in **A2**.
A7	1—4	Third woman does as first man did in **A2**.
	5—8	As in **A2**.

PICKING UP STICKS—*continued.*

MUSIC.		MOVEMENTS.
		SECOND PART.
A1	1—4	Sides all.
	5 – 8	That again.
A2	1—8	First man and first woman face, take both hands, and go four slips down between second man and second woman ; while second man and second woman go four slips up into the top place (2 bars).
		Second man and second woman take both hands and slip down to places between first man and first woman ; while first man and first woman slip up to places (2 bars).
		First and second couples repeat these movements (4 bars).
		Simultaneously, third man and third woman cross over, cast up to the top, cross over again and cast down to places (sk.s).
A3	1—8	Third and second couples do as first and second couples did in A2, third couple first slipping up between second man and second woman ; while first man and first woman cross over, cast down to the bottom, cross over again and cast up to places.
		THIRD PART.
A1	1—4	Partners arm with the right.
	5—8	Partners arm with the left.

PICKING UP STICKS—*continued.*

MUSIC.	MOVEMENTS.
	THIRD PART—*continued.*
A2, A3, and **A4**	First man, followed by second and third men, crosses over and threads or heys through the three women (they standing still), passing outside first woman, inside second, and outside third. The first and second men, on reaching the third woman, pass, clockwise, completely round her and face up; while the third man, instead of following second man round third woman, passes counter-clockwise completely round second woman and faces up, thus becoming the head of the file (sk.s.).
	Third man, followed by first and second men, then heys up to the top, the second man (now the hindermost), instead of following first man round first woman, passing counter-clockwise round second woman, and facing down.
	The three, now led by second man, then hey once again to the bottom, the first man (now the hindermost) passing counter-clockwise completely round second woman and facing up.
	Led by first man, the three, now in their proper order, hey up to the top, turn to their right, cast down to the bottom, and then move up to their respective places.
A5, A6, and **A7.**	The women do as the men did in A2, A3, and A4.

SCOTCH CAP.

Longways for six ; in three parts (1st Ed., 1650).

MUSIC.		MOVEMENTS.
		Running-step throughout the dance.
		### FIRST PART.
A	1—4	All lead up a double and fall back a double to places.
	5—8	That again.
B1	1—4	First and second women and second and third men fall back two steps, cross over and change places, first woman with second man and second woman with third man.
	5—8	First man and third woman fall back two steps, cross over, and change places.
B2	1—8	All that again to places.
		### SECOND PART.
A	1—4	Partners side.
	5—8	That again.
B1	1—4	The men take hands, fall back a double and move forward a double to places; while the women do the same.
	5—8	First & third men, first & third women, second man & second woman, arm with the right and fall back to places.
B2	1—4	As in B1.
	5—8	Partners turn.

SCOTCH CAP—*continued.*

MUSIC.		MOVEMENTS.
		THIRD PART.
A	1—4	Partners arm with the right.
	5—8	Partners arm with the left.
B1	1—2	The men go four slips up, while the women go four slips down, so that third man faces first woman.
	3—8	Progressive hey, handing, three changes, to places, third man and first woman beginning the movement. (*In the third and last change, second man turns his partner once round with the right hand, while first and third men turn their partners three-quarters round.*)
B2	1—8	Same movement as in B1, except that the men slip down and the women slip up, and that first man and third woman begin the progressive hey.

GREENWOOD.

Longways for six; in six parts (1st Ed. **1650**).

① ② ③

1 ② 3

MUSIC.		MOVEMENTS.
		FIRST PART.
A1	1—4	All facing front, move forward a double and fall back a double to places.
	5—8	Partners set and turn single.
A2	1—4	The second man leads the first and third women out a double, changes hands and leads them back a double to places; while the second woman does the same with the first and third men.
	5—8	Partners set and turn single.
A3	1—4	Second man sides with his partner; while first man sides with third man, and first woman with third woman.
	5—8	Partners set and turn single.
A4	1—4	First man sides with second woman, and second man with first woman; while third man sides with his partner.
	5—8	Partners set and turn single.
A5	1—4	Second man sides with third woman, and third man with second woman; while first man sides with his partner.
	5—8	Partners set and turn single.

GREENWOOD— *continued.*

MUSIC.		MOVEMENTS.
		SECOND PART.
A1 and **A2**		As in First Part.
A3 and **A4**		As in First Part, except that the dancers arm with the right instead of siding.
A5	1—8	As in First Part, except that the dancers arm with the left instead of siding.
		THIRD PART.
A1 and **A2**		As in First Part.
A3	1—4	Each file hands-three.
	5—8	Partners set and turn single.
A4	1—4	First couple and second man hands-three; while third couple and second woman do the same.
	5—8	Partners set and turn single.
A5	1—4	Third couple and second man hands-three; while first couple and second woman do the same.
	5—8	Partners set and turn single.
		FOURTH PART.
A1 and **A2**		As in First Part.
A3	1—8	Each file goes the whole-hey.
A4	1—8	First woman moves forward between first and second men and all three go the whole-hey, second man and first woman passing by the right.
		Simultaneously, third man moves forward between second and third women and all three go the whole-hey, third man and second woman passing by the right.

GREENWOOD—*continued.*

MUSIC.		MOVEMENTS.
		FOURTH PART—*continued.*
A5	1—8	First man moves forward between first and second women, and all three go the whole-hey, first man facing second woman and passing by the left.
		Simultaneously, third woman moves forward between second and third men, and all three go the whole-hey, third woman and second man facing and passing by the left.
		FIFTH PART.
A1 and **A2**		As in First Part.
A3	1—4	The three men go hands-three round second woman.
	5—8	Partners set and turn single.
A4	1—4	The three women go hands-three round second man.
	5—8	Partners set and turn single.
		SIXTH PART.
A1 and **A2**		As in First Part.
A3	1—8	The second woman falling back, the three men go the whole-hey, second man moving between first and third men and passing the latter by the right.
A4	1—8	The second man falling back, the three women go the whole-hey, second woman moving between the first and third women and passing the former by the right.
A5 and **A6**		Same as A1 and A2 in First Part.

STEP STATELY.

Longways for three, five, seven or nine couples ; in three
parts (1st Ed. 1650).

MUSIC.		MOVEMENTS.
		FIRST PART.
A	1—2	All lead up a double.
	3—4	Still facing up, men go four slips to their right behind their partners ; while the women go four slips to their left.
	5—8	The men face the right wall and join hands, while the women face the left wall and do likewise. The first man, followed by the other men, casts down to the bottom of the Set and stands with the rest of the men in a straight line on his right hand, all facing the Presence ; while the women, in like manner, led by first woman, cast down and stand in line with the men, first woman next to first man.
B	1—4	All take hands, move up a double and fall back a double.
	5—8	First man and first woman having released their hands, the women, hand-in-hand, move to the right in front of the men and dance up to places ; while the men move to the left and do the same.

STEP STATELY—*continued.*

MUSIC.		MOVEMENTS.

SECOND PART.

(Duple minor-set.)

A	1—4	First man and first woman lead up a double, change hands, and lead back to places.
	5—6	First and second couples hands-four half-way round (r.s.).
	7—8	First man and second woman change places.
B	1—4	First and second women lead up to the top, cross over and stand, the first woman behind the second man, the second woman behind the first man.
	5—8	The two men, giving right hands, pass each other, and then turn their partners with left hands, the first couple falling into the second place, the second couple into the first place (progressive) (sk.s.).

THIRD PART.

(Progressive.)

A	1—4	First man and first woman cross over, cast down and cross again in the second place, the second couple moving up to the top.
	5—6	The first three men taking hands, the first three women doing the same, all move forward a double, first man and first woman meeting, second and third men changing places with their partners.
	7—8	The two files fall back a double.
B	1—4	First man and first woman lead up to the top and then, followed by second couple, cast down into the third place, second couple falling into the second place, and third couple moving up into the first place.
	5—8	Second and third couples hands-four half-way round ; while first man and first woman arm with the right (progressive)

STEP STATELY—*continued.*

*When three couples only are dancing, the progressive movement
is that of an ordinary Whole-set dance. When,
however, five, seven or nine couples are dancing, the
progressive movement is that of a triple minor-set
with this difference that the leading couples gain
two places in each round instead of one. In this
latter case, couples going up the dance should be
careful to note at the beginning of each round to
which minor-set they belong and their place in that
set. This they can most easily do by carefully noting
the positions and movements of the leading couples.
It should be noted that the restriction with regard to
the number of the performers is operative in the
Third Part only.*

AYE ME, OR, THE SYMPHONY.

Longways for eight ; in three parts (1st Ed. 1650).

MUSIC.		MOVEMENTS.
		Running-step throughout the dance.
		FIRST PART.
A1	1—4	Partners lead up a double and fall back a double to places.
	5—6	Partners face ; men fall back two steps in fifth bar, women the same in sixth bar.
	7—8	All move forward to places, turning single as they do so.
A2	1—8	All that again.
B1	1—4	First man and first woman cast down, meet below the second couple and change places ; while fourth man and fourth woman cast up, meet above the third couple and change places.
	5—8	First man and first woman cast up to the top, cross over and move down into the second place, the first man taking second man by both hands and turning him counter clockwise up into the first place, the first woman in like manner turning second woman clockwise into the first place. Simultaneously, fourth and third couples do likewise.
B2	1—8	All that again to places, second and third couples initiating the movement.

AYE ME—*continued.*

MUSIC.		MOVEMENTS.
		SECOND PART.
A1	1—4	Partners honour (2 bars) and change places, passing by the *left* (2 bars).
	5 - 6	Men fall back two steps in fifth bar, women the same in sixth bar.
	7---8	All move forward a double to places, turning single as they do so.
A2	1—8	All that again to places.
B1	1—2	All face up. First and third men and women go four slips outward; while second and fourth men and women go four slips inward.
	3—4	First and third couples fall back a double; while second and fourth couples move up a double.
	5---6	Still facing up, first and third men and women go four slips inward; while second and fourth men and women go four slips outward.
	7 - 8	First and third couples move forward a double; while second and fourth couples fall back a double.
B2	1—2	As in B1, all facing down.
	3—4	First and third couples move forward a double; while second and fourth couples fall back a double.
	5 - 6	As in B1, all facing down.
	7—8	First and third couples fall back a double to places; while second and fourth couples move forward a double to places.

AYE ME—*continued.*

MUSIC.		MOVEMENTS.

THIRD PART.

A1 1—4 | Partners arm with the right once-and-a-half round, and change places.

5—6 | Men fall back two steps in fifth bar ; the women doing the same in sixth bar.

7 – 8 | All move forward a double, turning single as they do so.

A2 1—4 | Partners arm with the left once-and-a-half round to places.

5—8 | As in A1 to places.

B1 1—4 | Second and third couples cast off and move into first and fourth places respectively. Simultaneously, first and fourth couples face, move forward, meet, change places (opposites passing by the right), and stay in the third and second stations respectively. Whereupon, first and fourth men change places with their partners.

5—6 | First man with his right hand takes the fourth man by the left and changes places with him, both moving counter-clockwise ; while first woman with her left hand takes the fourth woman by the right and changes places with her, both moving clockwise.

7—8 | First and fourth men change places with their partners.

B2 1—8 | Movement repeated to places, first and fourth couples casting off, while second and third couples meet, pass each other, etc

PRINCE RUPERT'S MARCH.

Longways for eight; in three parts (1st Ed. 1650).

MUSIC.		MOVEMENTS.
		Walking-step throughout the dance.
		First Part.
A	1—8	First couple, followed by second, third and fourth couples, leads round to the right to the bottom and then up the middle to places.
B1	1—4	First man, followed by second, third and fourth men, crosses over, moves down outside the women and stands behind fourth woman.
	5—6	All face left wall and move forward a double.
	7—8	Men change places with the women opposite them.
B2	1—4	As in B1, fourth man leading the other men.
	5—6	As in B1.
	7—8	Partners change places.
		Second Part.
A	1—8	First couple, followed by the remaining three couples, leads round to the left to the bottom and then up the middle to places.
B1 and **B2**		The women do as the men did in the First Part, moving down behind the men, advancing toward the right wall, etc.

PRINCE RUPERT'S MARCH—*continued*.

MUSIC.		MOVEMENTS.
		THIRD PART.
A	1—8	As in First Part.
B1	1—4	The first man, followed by the other three men, crosses over and moves down to the bottom on the women's side ; while the fourth woman, followed by the other three women, crosses over and moves up to the top on the men's side (*i.e.*, all move round clockwise).
	5—8	Partners face. All fall back a double and move forward a double.
B2	1—4	Movement in B1 repeated in reverse, the men headed by fourth man, the women headed by first woman moving down and up respectively to places (*i.e.*, all moving round counter-clockwise).
	5—8	As in B1.

THE HEALTH; OR, THE MERRY WASSAIL.

Longways for eight; in three parts (1st Ed. 1650).

| 1 | 2 | 3 | 4 |

| ① | ② | ③ | ④ |

MUSIC.		MOVEMENTS.
		FIRST PART.
A1	1—4	All lead up a double and fall back a double to places.
	5—8	Partners set-and-honour.
A2	1—8	All that again.
A3	1—4	First and fourth couples face each other, meet and go back to-back, staying in the second and third places respectively; while second couple casts up into the first place, and third couple casts down into the fourth place (r.s.).
	5—8	First man and first woman cast up to the top, and return down the middle to the same places; while fourth man and fourth woman cast down to the bottom, and return up the middle to the same places (r.s.).
A4	1—8	Movement repeated to places, second and third couples meeting, going back-to-back, etc.

THE HEALTH—*continued.*

MUSIC.		MOVEMENTS.
		SECOND PART.
A1	1—4	Hands-all, half-way round, facing outward (r.s.).
	5—8	Partners set-and-honour.
A2	1—4	Hands-all, half-way round, counter-clockwise, facing outward to places (r.s.).
	5—8	Partners set-and-honour.
A3	1—4	As in A3, First Part.
	5—8	First and fourth couples hands-four, facing outward (r.s.).
A4	1—8	As in A3, second and third couples meeting, going back-to-back, etc.
		THIRD PART.
A1	1—4	Partners turn once-and-a-half round and change places (sk.s.).
	5—6	First and second men, third and fourth men, first and second women, and third and fourth women turn half-way round and change places (sk.s.).
	7—8	Partners set.
A2	1—8	All that again to places.

THE HEALTH—*continued.*

MUSIC.		MOVEMENTS.
		THIRD PART—*continued.*
A3	1—4	First and fourth couples face each other and meet; while second and third couples cast up and down respectively into first and fourth places (r.s.).
	5—8	First and fourth men and women clap their hands and go right-hands across.
A4	1—8	Movement repeated to places, second and third couples meeting, clapping hands, etc.
		Alternative Version.
A3	1—2	First man and fourth woman move forward, meet and join right hands; while second man casts up into first place and third woman casts down into fourth place (r.s. .
	3—4	First woman and fourth man move forward, meet and join right hands; while second woman casts up into first place and third man casts down into fourth place.
	5—8	First and fourth couples right-hands-across once round.
A4	1—8	Movement continued to places, second man and third woman meeting, joining hands, etc.

HALFE HANNIKIN.

Longways for as many as will; in one part (1st Ed. **1650**).

| 1 | 2 | 3 | 4 | . . . . . |
| ① | ② | ③ | ④ | . . . . . |

MUSIC.		MOVEMENTS.
		(Progressive.)
A	1—4	All lead up a double and fall back a double to places.
	5—8	That again.
B1	1—4	Opposites side.
	5—8	The top dancer on the men's side and the bottom dancer on the women's side turn their opposites and then fall out, the former standing neutral at the top, and on the right of the General Set, the latter at the bottom and on the left; while the rest of the dancers on the men's side turn their opposites and move up one place.
		All (with the exception of the two neutral dancers) are now facing up in couples, second man with first woman, third man with second woman, and so forth.
A2	1—4	All the couples lead up a double and fall back a double to places.
	5—8	That again.
B2	1—4	Opposites side.

HALFE HANNIKIN—*continued.*

MUSIC.	MOVEMENTS.
5—8	All the dancers on the women's side turn their opposites and move down one place, the neutral dancer at the top moving into the vacant place at the top of the women's side, and the neutral dancer at the bottom into the vacant place at the bottom of the men's side (progressive).

The above movements are then repeated, and the dance proceeds until all the men have changed over to the women's side (first man at the lower end), and all the women have changed over to the men's side (last woman at the upper end); or, if preferred, until all are once again in their original places.

THE COLLIER'S DAUGHTER; OR, THE DUKE OF RUTLAND'S DELIGHT.

Longways for as many as will; in one part (Vol. 2, 4th Ed. 1728).

1	2	3	4	. . . .
①	②	③	④	• • • •

MUSIC.		MOVEMENTS.
		(Triple minor-set.)
A1	1—4	First man and first woman cross over and cast down into second place (improper), second couple moving up into first place.
	5— 8	First man turns first woman.
A2	1—4	First man and first woman cross over and cast down into the third place (proper), third couple moving up into the second place.
	5—8	First man turns first woman.
B1	1—2	First man leads first woman up the middle into the second place, third couple moving down into the third place (progressive).
	3—6	First and second couples hands-four.
	7—8	All four turn single.
B2	1—4	First and second couples circular-hey, four changes, partners facing.
	5—8	First and second men turn their partners.

UP GOES ELY.

Longways for as many as will; in one part (Vol 3, *c.* 1728).

MUSIC.		MOVEMENTS.
		N.B.—*The tune is in triple time, i.e., three steps to the bar.* *Running-step throughout the dance.* (Triple minor-set.)
A	1—4	First man and first woman cast off into the second place (second couple moving up into the first place), turn each other half-way round and change places (improper), cast off again and meet below the third couple.
	5—8	First man and first woman lead up the middle to the top and cast off into the second place (still improper).
B	1—2	First man moves into the middle and, facing down, goes hands-three with the third couple half-way round ; while first woman, facing up, does the same with the second couple.
		Second and third men have now changed places with their partners; while first woman is standing above the second couple, facing down, and first man below the third couple, facing up.
	3—4	First man and first woman meet, turn half-way round and fall back, each into the other's place.

UP GOES ELY—*continued.*

MUSIC.	MOVEMENTS.
5—6	First man (standing above second couple, facing down) goes hands-three with second couple half-way round ; while first woman (standing below third couple, facing up) does the same with third couple.
7—8	Second and third men turn their partners; while first man and first woman face, turn three-quarters round and fall into the second place (progressive ; proper).

EVERY LAD HIS LASS.

Longways for as many as will; in one part
(Vol. 2, 4th Ed. 1728).

MUSIC.		MOVEMENTS.
		(Triple minor-set.)
A	1—4	First man and first woman set and cast down into second place, second couple moving up into first place.
	5—8	Second couple set and cast down into second place, first couple moving up into first place.
B	1—2	First man and second woman meet with two steps and a jump on the two beats of the first bar and the first beat of the second, respectively.
	3—4	First woman and second man meet in like manner.
	5—6	All four return to places, turning single as they do so.
	7—12	First man and first woman cross over, cast down, meet below second couple, cross over again, cast down, meet below third couple, and move up the middle into the second place; while second couple moves up into first place (progressive).

EPSOM NEW WELLS.

Longways for as many as will; in one part
(Vol. 2, 4th Ed. 1728).

1	2	3	4	. . . .
①	②	③	④	. . . .

MUSIC.		MOVEMENTS.

(Triple minor-set.)

A 1—4 | First man turns second woman half-way round. First man then passes clockwise round second man and returns to his place; while second woman passes clockwise round first woman and returns to her place.

5—8 | First woman turns second man half-way round. First woman then passes clockwise round first man and returns to her place; while second man passes clockwise round second woman and returns to his place.

B1 1—8 | First man and first woman lead down the middle, while second man and second woman cast up and then follow behind them. First and second couples lead through the third couple, cast up, men to their right and women to their left, and return to places.

B2 1—4 | First and second men lead a double to the left wall, change hands, and lead a double back again to places; while first and second women lead to the right wall and back again in like manner.

5—6 | Partners set.

7—8 | First man and first woman cast down into second place, second couple moving up into first place (progressive).

MY LADY'S COURANT.

Longways for as many as will; in one part
(Vol. 2, 4th Ed. 1728).

1	2	3	4	. . . .
(1)	(2)	(3)	(4)	. . . .

MUSIC.		MOVEMENTS.
		(Triple minor-set.)
A1	1—4	First man and first woman cast down into the second place, second couple moving up into first place.
	5—8	Second couple and first man hands-three once round, while third couple and first woman do the same.
A2	1—8	First man and first woman cast up to the top, cross over, cast down and hands-three once round, the man with second and third women, the woman with second and third men. *The first couple is now in the second place (improper).*
B1	1—4	First woman moves up the middle and passes clockwise round second woman to the second place on her own side; while first man moves up the middle and passes counter-clockwise round second man to the second place on his own side.

MY LADY'S COURANT—*continued.*

MUSIC.	MOVEMENTS.
5—8	First man and first woman turn each other and then cast up into the first place, second couple moving down into the second place.
B2 1—6	First man, taking his partner's left hand in his right—she taking the second woman's left hand in her right—casts off to his left, and, followed by first and second women, goes a complete circle, counter-clockwise, round second man.
7—8	First man and first woman cast down into the second place, second couple moving up into the first place (progressive).

ORLEANS BAFFLED.

Longways for as many as will; in one part
(Vol. 2, 4th Ed. 1728).

MUSIC.		MOVEMENTS.
		N.B.—*The tune is in triple time, i.e., three steps to the bar.*
		Running-step throughout the dance.
		(Triple minor-set.)
A	1—2	First man and first woman cast down into second place, second couple moving up into first place.
	3—4	First and third couples half-poussette and change places (first man pushing and then pulling).
	5—6	First man and first woman cast up into second place, third couple moving down into the third place.
	7—8	First and second couples half-poussette and change places (first man pulling and then pushing).
	Bar 9	First man and second woman change places.
	Bar 10	Second man and first woman change places.
	11—12	First and second couples circular-hey, three changes, men facing and women facing (progressive).

A TRIP TO KILBURN.

Longways for as many as will; in one part
(Vol. 2, 4th Ed. 1728).

1	2	3	4	• • • •
①	②	③	④	• • • •

MUSIC.		MOVEMENTS.
		(Triple minor-set.)
A1	1—2	First man and first woman cast down into second place, second couple moving up into first place.
	3—6	First and third couples hands-four.
	7—8	First couple leads through third couple.
A2	1—2	First man and first woman cast up into the second place.
	3—6	First and second couples hands-four.
	7—8	First couple leads through second couple.
B1	1—2	First man and first woman cast off into second place (progressive).
	3—8	First, second and third couples hands-six.
B2	1—4	First and second couples circular-hey, four changes, partners facing.
	5—8	First and second men turn their partners.

MY LADY WINWOOD'S MAGGOT.

Longways for as many as will; in one part
(Vol. 3, *c.* 1728).

| 1 | 2 | 3 | 4 | . . . . |
| ① | ② | ③ | ④ | . . . . |

MUSIC.		MOVEMENTS.
		(Triple minor-set.)
A1	1—4	First man and first woman set and cast down into second place, second couple moving up into first place.
	5—8	First man and first woman lead through the third couple and cast up into second place (progressive).
A2	1—8	First man goes figure of eight with third couple, passing counter-clockwise round the third woman and clockwise round the third man; while first woman does the same with second couple, passing counter-clockwise round second man and clockwise round second woman (sk.s.).
B1	1—4	First, second and third couples hands-six.
	5—8	First, second and third men go back-to-back with their partners.
B2	1—4	First man and first woman lead down through third couple, cast up to the top and lead down the middle to the second place.
	5—8	First man turns his partner.

THE MAIDEN'S BLUSH.

Longways for as many as will; in one part
(Vol. 2, 4th Ed. 1728).

MUSIC.		MOVEMENTS.
		(Triple minor-set.)
A	1— 4	First man and first woman set and cast down into second place, second couple moving up into first place.
	5—8	Same again, first couple changing places with third couple.
B1	1—4	First man and first woman lead up to the top, and cast down into second place, third couple moving down into third place.
	5—8	First and second couples circular-hey, two changes, partners facing.
B2	1—4	First and second men turn their partners.
	5—8	First and second couples circular-hey, two changes, partners facing (progressive).

JENNY, COME TIE MY CRAVAT.

Longways for as many as will ; in two parts (8th Ed. 1690)

| 1 | 2 | 3 | 4 | . . . . |

| ① | ② | ③ | ④ | . . . . |

MUSIC.		MOVEMENTS.
		FIRST PART.
		(Triple minor-set.)
A	1—4	First man turns second woman.
	5—8	First woman turns second man.
B	1—8	First man and first woman cross over, cast down, cross over below the second couple, cast down again, meet below the third couple, lead up the middle to the top, and cast down into second place, second couple moving up into first place (progressive).
		SECOND PART.
		(Duple minor-set.)
A	1—2	First and second women fall back a double, while first and second men move forward a double.
	3—4	All four turn single.

JENNY, COME TIE MY CRAVAT—*continued.*

MUSIC.	MOVEMENTS.
	Second Part— *continued.*
5— 6	The two men fall back a double, and the two women move forward a double to places.
7—8	All four turn single.
B 1— 4	Partners side, all clapping their hands on the first beat of the first bar.
5—6	All four turn single.
7—8	First man and first woman cast down into second place, while second couple moves up into first place, partners striking each other's hands (right on left and left on right) on the first beat of the bar (progressive).

MR. ISAAC'S MAGGOT.

Longways for as many as will; in one part (9th Ed. 1695).

| 1 | 2 | 3 | 4 | . . . . |

| ① | ② | ③ | ④ | . . . . |

MUSIC.	MOVEMENTS.
	N.B.---*The tune is in triple-time ; i.e., three steps to the bar.*
	(Duple minor-set.)
A 1 — 4	First man turns second woman with the right hand and returns clockwise round second man to his place.
5—8	First woman turns second man with the left hand and returns counter-clockwise round second woman to her place.
B 1—4	First and second men take hands, fall back six steps and move forward to places, turning single in the last three steps as they do so ; while first and second women do the same.
5—8	First and second couples circular-hey to places, four changes, partners facing. After the last change first man and first woman fall back and stand between second man and second woman, all four facing up.
9 - 10	First and second couples, four abreast, with linked hands, lead up three steps and fall back three steps.
11—12	First and second couple lead up three steps, the second couple staying in the first place, while first man and first woman cast down into the second place (progressive).

THE FIT'S COME ON ME NOW.

Longways for as many as will ; in one part (7th Ed. 1686).

1		2		3		4		•	•	•	•

①		②		③		④		•	•	-	•

MUSIC.		MOVEMENTS.
		N.B.—*The tune is in triple time, i.e., three steps to the bar.*
		(Duple minor-set.)
A	1—2	First man casts down, passes below second man and returns up the middle to his place ; while the second woman moves up the middle, casts down and returns to her place.
	3—4	First and second men turn their partners.
	5—6	First woman casts down, passes below the second woman and returns up the middle to her place ; while the second man moves up the middle, casts down and returns to his place.
	7—8	First and second men turn their partners.
B	Bar 1	First and second men change places with their partners.
	2—4	First woman and first man cross over and move down between second couple, cast up to their original places, and turn single.
	Bar 5	Second man and second woman cast up to the first place (improper), first couple moving down to second place (progressive).
	6—8	Second man and second woman cross over and move down between first couple, cast up into the first place, and turn single.

THE CORONATION DAY.

Longways for as many as will ; in one part
(10th Ed. 1698).

1	2	3	4	• • • •
①	②	③	④	• • • •

MUSIC.		MOVEMENTS.
		(Duple minor-set.)
A	1—4	First man with his right hand takes his partner by her left hand and leads her down the middle, passing her before him into second man's place, he falling into second woman's place; while second man and second woman cast up to the top, cross over and change sides.
	5— 8	Second man with his left hand takes his partner by her right hand, and leads her down the middle into the second place, passing her before him on to her own side ; while first man and first woman cast up to the top, cross over and change sides.
B1	1—4	First man moves round his partner counter-clockwise into her place, while she (in bars 3 and 4) moves down into second woman's place, turning single as she does so. Simultaneously, second woman passes counter-clockwise round her partner into his place, while he (in bars 3 and 4) moves up into first man's place, turning single. clockwise, as he does so.

THE CORONATION DAY.—*continued.*

MUSIC.		MOVEMENTS.
	5—8	First man and first woman lead to the left wall between second man and second woman, cast off and return to the same places.
B2	1—2	Second man casts down and crosses over into the second place on the women's side ; while first woman crosses over into the first place on the men's side.
	3—4	All four turn single.
	5—8	First man and first woman cross over and cast down into the second place ; while second man with his right hand takes his partner by her left hand and leads her up the middle, passing her before him into the first place on the women's side, he falling into the first place on the men's side (progressive).

LADY BANBURY'S HORNPIPE.

Longways for as many as will; in three parts (3rd Ed. 1665).

| 1 | 2 | 3 | 4 | . . . . |

| ① | ② | ③ | ④ | . . ○ . |

MUSIC.	MOVEMENTS.
	N.B.—*The tune is in triple time, i.e., three steps to the bar.**
	FIRST PART.
	(Duple minor-set.)
A 1—4	First man and first woman cast down into the second place, cross over and stand, first man on the outside of second woman (both facing down), first woman on the outside of second man (both facing up).
B 1—2	First man and second woman (taking inside hands) lead down three steps and fall back three steps; while second man and first woman (taking inside hands) lead up three steps and fall back three steps.
3—4	Second man and second woman go right-hands-across half-way round, holding first woman and first man respectively in their left hands. Upon the conclusion of this movement, first couple falls into second place, while second man changes places with second woman and both fall into the first place (progressive).

* Playford bars it, wrongly, as we believe, in duple time.

LADY BANBURY'S HORNPIPE— *continued.*

MUSIC.		MOVEMENTS.

SECOND PART.

(Duple minor-set.)

A 1—2 · The two men face and take both hands, the two women doing the same. First man pulls second man up three steps and pushes him down the middle three steps ; while the second woman pulls first woman down three steps and then pushes her up the middle three steps.
All four are now in line, second man and first woman back to back.

3—4 · First man and second woman change places, both moving to their left, *i.e.*, clockwise.

B 1—2 · Second man and first woman go three slips to their left—second man toward left wall, first woman toward right wall. Whereupon second woman and first man change places.

3—4 · First and second couples hands-across rather less than half-way round (three steps), and partners change places (progressive).

THIRD PART.

(Duple minor-set.)

A Bar 1 · First man moves forward and stands above his partner, both facing up.

LADY BANBURY'S HORNPIPE—*continued.*

MUSIC.	MOVEMENTS.
	THIRD PART—*continued.*
Bar 2	Second man in like manner moves in front of his partner.
3—4	All four move up three steps and fall back three steps (w.s.).
B Bar 1	The first man goes three slips to his right, while his partner goes three slips to her left.
Bar 2	Second man and second woman do the same.
Bar 3	First man and first woman cast down into the second place, second couple leading up into the first place.
Bar 4	First and second men change places with their partners (progressive).

CHRISTCHURCH BELLS.

Longways for as many as will ; in one part
(7th Ed. 1686).

MUSIC.		MOVEMENTS.
		(Duple minor-set.)
A	1—8	First man turns second woman with the right hand and then turns his partner with the left, falling back into his place.
B	1—8	Second man turns first woman with the left hand and then turns his partner with the right, falling back into his place.
C	1—4	First and second couples hands-four.
	Bar 5	On the first beat of the bar, all clap hands ; on the middle beat of the bar, partners strike right hands together.
	Bar 6	As in previous bar, except that, on the middle beat of the bar, partners strike left hands together.
	7—8	First man and first woman cast down into second place ; while second couple leads up into first place (progressive).

THE WHIM.

Longways for as many as will; in one part
(9th Ed. 1695).

MUSIC.		MOVEMENTS.
		(Duple minor-set.)
A	1—2	First and second men take hands and fall back a double; while first and second women do the same.
	3—6	Releasing hands, all four move forward, cross over, and change sides.
	7—12	Same again to places.
B	1—4	First and second men go back-to-back, while first and second women do the same.
	5—6	All four turn single.
	7—12	Circular-hey, three changes, partners facing, the first couple falling into the second place, the second couple into the first (progressive).

LOVE LIES A-BLEEDING.

Longways for as many as will; in one part (7th Ed. **1686**).

MUSIC.		MOVEMENTS.
		(Duple minor-set.)
A	1—4	First man and first woman cast down into the second place, and then go back-to-back, passing by the right ; while second couple moves up into the first place.
	5—8	First man and first woman cast up into the first place and then go back-to-back, passing by the left ; while second couple moves down into the second place.
B	Bar 1	On the first beat of the bar, first and second men clap hands and, on the middle beat, strike each other's hands (right on left and left on right); while the two women do the same.
	Bar 2	As in previous bar, except that, on the middle beat, *partners* strike each other's hands.
	3—4	First man and first woman cast down into the second place, second couple moving up into the first place (progressive).
	5—6	As in bars 1—2.
	7—8	Partners turn each other.

JACOB HALL'S JIG.

Longways for as many as will; in one part (9th Ed. 1695).

1	2	3	4	. . . .
①	②	③	④	• • • •

MUSIC.		MOVEMENTS.
		(Duple minor-set.)
A1	1—4	First man turns second woman with the right hand and then turns his partner with the left.
	5—8	First couple and second woman hands-three, counter-clockwise, to places.
A2	1—4	Second man turns first woman with the left hand and then turns his partner with the right.
	5—8	Second couple and first woman hands-three, clockwise, to places.
B1	1—4	First man and first woman lead down the middle, change hands, lead up and stand between second man and second woman, all four facing up.
	5—8	Taking hands, all four move up a double and fall back a double, first couple into second place, second couple into first place (progressive).
B2	1—4	First and second couples hands-four.
	5—8	First man and first woman lead up the middle, and cast down into second place.

THE TEMPLE CHANGE.

Longways for as many as will; in one part
(Vol. 2, 2nd Ed. 1698).

| 1 | 2 | 3 | 4 | • • • • |

| ① | ② | ③ | ④ | • • • • |

MUSIC.		MOVEMENTS.
		(Duple minor-set.)
A	1—2	First and second couples hands-four half-way round.
	3—4	All turn single.
	5—8	All that again.
B	1—2	First man and second woman change places.
	3—4	First woman and second man change places.
	5—6	Hands-four half-way round.
	7—8	First man and first woman cast down into second place, the second couple leading up into first place (progressive).

THE MARY AND DOROTHY.

Longways for as many as will; in one part
(Vol. 3, c. 1728).

1		2		3		4	. . . .
①		②		③		④	. . . .

MUSIC.		MOVEMENTS.
		(Duple minor-set.)
A	1—4	First and second couples set and turn single.
	5—8	First and second couples hands-four.
B	1—4	First man leads first woman a double down the middle, changes hands, and leads her a double up.
	5—6	First man and first woman cast down into second place, second couple moving up into first place (progressive).

JOG ON.

Longways for as many as will; in four parts
(1st Ed. 1650).

| 1 | 2 | 3 | 4 | • • • • |

| ① | ② | ③ | ④ | • • • • |

MUSIC.	MOVEMENTS.
	FIRST PART.
A1 1—4	All lead up a double and fall back a double to places.
5—8	Partners set and turn single.
A2 1 8	All that again.
	SECOND PART. (Duple minor-set.)
A 1—4	First man, with his back to the Presence, faces his partner and, taking her by both hands, falls back two steps and then pushes her down the middle between second man and second woman.
5—8	First man and second couple hands-three round first woman (first man standing on the right of second man), first couple falling into second place, second couple into first place (progressive).
	THIRD PART. (Duple minor-set.)
A 1—4	First man takes first woman by both hands, pushes her down behind second woman, and then into second man's place, he moving into second woman's place; while second couple moves up into the first place (progressive, improper).
5 – 8	First and second men turn their partners.
	In the next round, first man pushes his partner behind third man into third woman's place (progressive, proper).

JOG ON—*continued*.

MUSIC.	MOVEMENTS.
	FOURTH PART.
A　1—4	First man and first woman cast down and stand on the outside of second man and second woman respectively, all four facing up. Taking hands, all move up a double and fall back a double, the first couple into the second place, the second couple into the first (progressive).
5—8	First and second men arm their partners with the right.

THE MOCK HOBBY HORSE.

Longways for as many as will; in one part
(10th Ed. 1698).

1	2	3	4	• • • • •
①	②	③	④	• • • • •

MUSIC.		MOVEMENTS.
		(Duple minor-set.)
A	1—4	First man turns second woman.
	5—8	Second man turns first woman.
B1	1—4	First and second men take hands, move forward between first and second women and cast off to places, first man to his left, second man to his right.
	5—8	First and second men turn once-and-a-half round and change places; while first and second women do the same (progressive).
B2	1—4	Women do as men did in B1.
	5—8	Partners turn.

JUICE OF BARLEY.

Longways for as many as will; in one part
(8th Ed. 1690).

MUSIC.		MOVEMENTS.
		(Duple minor-set.)
A	1—4	First man and first woman go back-to-back; while second man and second woman do the same.
	5—8	Partners turn.
B1	1—4	First man, followed by second man, passes between first and second woman, turns to his right into second place, second man turning to his left into first place.
	5—8	All clap hands on the first beat of the fifth bar and go hands-four once round.
B2	1—4	First woman, followed by second woman, passes between first and second men, turns to her left into second place, second woman turning to her right into first place (progressive).
	5—8	As in B1.

MAIDS' MORRIS.

Longways for as many as will; in one part
(8th Ed. 1690).

MUSIC.		MOVEMENTS.
		(Duple minor-set.)
A	1—4	First and second men take hands, fall back a double, and then move forward a double to places, turning single as they do so.
	5—8	First and second women do the same.
B1	1—2	First and second couples hands-four four slips clockwise.
	3—4	All four turn single.
	5—6	First and second couples hands-four four slips counter-clockwise to places.
	7—8	All turn single.
B2	1—6	Circular-hey to places, four changes, partners facing.
		First man leads first woman down the middle into second place; while second man and second woman cast up into the first place (progressive).

LILLI BURLERO.

Longways for as many as will ; in one part (8th Ed. 1690).

	MUSIC.	MOVEMENTS.
		(Duple minor set.)
A	1—4	First man and first woman lead down the middle below second couple, cast up and return to places.
	5—8	Second man and second woman lead up the middle, cast down and return to places.
B1	1—2	First man and second woman change places.
	3—4	First woman and second man change places.
	5—6	All fall back a double.
	7—8	All move forward a double, turning single as they do so.
B2	1—2	First and second men cross over and change places with their partners.
	3—4	First and second men move backward each into the other's place : while first and second women do the same.
	5—8	Circular-hey, three changes, partners facing (progressive).

POOL'S HOLE.

Longways for as many as will; in one part (8th Ed. 1690).

MUSIC.		MOVEMENTS.
		(Duple minor-set.)
A	1—4	First man and first woman cast down into the second place, second couple moving up into the first place. First woman then passes counter-clockwise round second man into the second place on the men's side; while first man passes clockwise round second woman into the second place on the women's side.
	5—6	First and second men change places.
	7—8	First and second women change places.
B	1—4	First and second couples hands-four.
	5—8	First and second couples progressive-hey, three changes, first man and first woman beginning the movement by passing by the right (progressive).

KING OF POLAND.

Longways for as many as will; in one part
(10th Ed. 1698).

1		2		3		4	• • • •
①		②		③		④	• • • •

MUSIC.		MOVEMENTS.
		(Duple minor-set.)
		Throughout this dance the leading couples are improper. Partners on reaching the top or bottom of the Set must therefore remember to change places.
A	1—4	The first couple being improper, first man and second woman turn once-and-a-half round and change places; while second man and first woman do the same.
	5—8	First and second men cross over and change places with their partners, and then, turning their partners half-way round, fall back to the same places.
B1	1—2	First couple leads up to the top; while second man and second woman cast down into the second place.
	3—6	Circular-hey, three changes, partners facing (progressive; improper).
B2	1—6	First woman and first man cross between second man and second woman and pass, the first woman clockwise round second woman, the first man counter-clockwise round second man, meet, turn half-way round and fall back to places.

THE COUNTRY DANCE BOOK.—PART II.

Music.		Movements.
		MAGE ON A CREE. *p.* 54.
		THIRD PART.
A3	1—4	Each man turns the woman on his left once round, and moves round one place clockwise (sk.s.).
	5—8	Each man turns the next woman once round and moves round another place clockwise (sk.s.).
		NEWCASTLE. *p.* 58.
		FIRST PART.
B1	3—8	Substitute "(r.s.)" for "(sk.s.)."
B2	1—2	Partners link left arms and swing round once (r.s.).
	3—8	Women right-hands-across clockwise to places (r.s.), while men dance round them counter-clockwise to places (sk.s.).
		SECOND PART.
A1	5—6	Partners go a single to the right and honour.
	7—8	Partners change places passing by the left (r.s.).
		THIRD PART.
B1	5—8	All turn single and change places with opposites, passing by the right (r.s.).
		ORANGES AND LEMONS. *p.* 65.
		THIRD PART.
A	5—8	Add "and first and third men lead their partners forward to face second and fourth couples respectively."
B1	3—6	First and second couples hands-four, half-way round, while third and fourth couples do the same. Second and fourth couples, men leading their partners, fall back into first and third couples' places respectively; simultaneously first and third couples lead forward and face fourth and second couples (*i.e.*, second and fourth couples move on one place counter-clockwise and take up positions facing centre; while first and third couples move on one place clockwise and take up positions with their backs to the centre).
		First and fourth couples hands-four, half-way round; while second and third couples do the same. Movement continued as in bars 3-6.

DULL SIR JOHN. *p.* 68.

Music.		Movements.
		FIRST PART.
A1	3—4	For "third man and third woman" read "fourth man and fourth woman."
		THIRD PART.
B1	1—4	First and third men go back-to-back with their opposites, passing by the right (r.s.).

PARSON'S FAREWELL. *p.* 74.

		SECOND PART.
A	7—8	All release hands and partners fall back to places, holding right hands.
B1	3—4	Substitute "(sk.s.)" for "(r.s.)."
	7—?	Substitute "(sk.s.)" for "(r.s.)."
		THIRD PART.
B1	1—2	Add "(sk.s.)."

ST. MARTIN'S. *p.* 81.

		FIRST PART.
B1	3—8	Men move forward and meet, take left hands and change places.
		First man then turns second woman once-and-a-half round with his right hand and changes places with her; while second man does the same with the first woman (sk.s.).
B2	3—8	Women move forward and meet, take left hands and change places.
		Partners turn once-and-a-half round with right hands and change places (sk.s.).
		SECOND PART.
A1	1—4	The two couples take two steps backward and then cross over and change places (r.s.).
		THIRD PART.
B1	5—8	Substitute "(r.s.)" for "(sk.s.)."
B2	5—6	Substitute "(r.s.)" for "(sk.s.)."
	7—8	All face up in line, taking hands (first couple on the right), move forward a double and honour the Presence (r.s.).

HEY, BOYS, UP GO WE. *p.* 85.

Music.		Movements.
		THIRD PART.
B1	5—8	Substitute "(r.s.)" for "(sk.s.)."
B2	5—8	Substitute "(r.s.)" for "(sk.s.)."

GRIMSTOCK. *p.* 88.

		THIRD PART.
B	Bar 1	Add "passing by the left."
	Bar 5	Add "passing by the right."

THE BEGGAR BOY. *p.* 90.

		FIRST PART.
B1	5—8	Substitute "once round" for "half-way round."

		THIRD PART.
B1	5—8	Substitute "(r.s.)" for "(sk.s.)."

CHESTNUT. *p.* 92.

		FIRST PART.
B1	2—4	Partners cross over, change places, and face each other (r.s.).

		SECOND PART.
A	1—4	Partners side.
	5—8	That again.
B1	5—8	Substitute "(r.s.)" for "(sk.s.)."

		THIRD PART.
	1—4	Partners arm with the right.
	5—8	Partners arm with the left.
B2	5—8	Substitute "(r.s.)" or "(sk.s.)."

THE BLACK NAG. *p.* 94.

		SECOND PART.
B1	1—2	Add "right shoulders foremost, passing back to back."

		THIRD PART.
B2	1—8	Add "while men turn single during the last two bars."

NONESUCH. $p.$ 101.

Music.	Movements.
	SECOND PART.
A1 1—4	(Duple minor-set.)
	First man and first woman face and move forward two steps; joining hands, they slip down between second man and second woman; releasing hands, first man turns clockwise to face second man, while first woman turns counter-clockwise to face second woman.
5—8	First man takes second man by both hands and pushes him obliquely upward and outward four steps, and then draws backward four steps, leaving second man in the top place, he himself falling into the second place (r.s.); simultaneously, first and second women do the same (progressive).
	THIRD PART.
B1 Bar 1	For "slips" read "springs on to his left foot."
Bar 2	For "slips" read "springs on to her left foot."
	FIFTH PART.
A1 Bar 1	For "slips" read "springs on to his right foot."
Bar 2	For "slips" read "springs on to her right foot."
B1 and **B2**	Substitute "(r.s.)" for "(sk.s.)."

MY LADY CULLEN. $p.$ 120.

	SECOND PART.
A1 1—4	For "First man and second woman" read "First man and first woman."

THE COUNTRY DANCE BOOK.—PART III.

IF ALL THE WORLD WERE PAPER.   *p.* 30.
Running-step throughout the dance.

CHELSEA REACH.   *p.* 36.

Music.		Movements.
		FIRST PART.
B2	5—8	(Alternative version.)
		Substitute "once" for "twice."
		THIRD PART.
A2	1—4	Each man, taking the woman on his left by the right hand, leads out a double and falls back a double (r.s.).
	5—8	Circular-hey, handing, half-way round, each man passing the woman whose hand he holds by the right (sk.s.). Each man is now face to face with the woman he led out.

HYDE PARK.   *p.* 44.

		FIRST PART.
B1	1—2	First man and first woman take two steps back, move forward and meet, and take both hands ; while third man and third woman do the same.

HUNSDON HOUSE.   *p.* 47.

		THIRD PART.
B1	5—8	Substitute " (r.s.) " for "(sk.s.)."

ARGEERS.   *p.* 51.

		SECOND PART.
B2	1—2	The two women move forward a double and meet.
	3—8	The two women fall back a double to places (r.s.) ; while the two men pass each other by the right, go counter-clockwise round their contrary partners, pass each other by the left, and go clockwise round their own partners, and return to places (sk.s.).
		THIRD PART.
B2	1—4	Substitute " (sk.s.) " for " (r.s.)."

LADY IN THE DARK. $p.$ 54.

Music.		Movements.
		FIRST PART.
A3	1—4	The two men meet and arm with the right (r.s.).
	5—8	Each man turns the contrary woman with the left hand, and returns to his place (r.s.).
A4	1—8	As in A3 1-8, the two women arming left and turning the contrary men with right hands (r.s.).

THE MERRY CONCEIT. $p.$ 57.

		SECOND PART.
A	1—4	Substitute "(sk.s.)" for "(r.s.)."

ADSON'S SARABAND. $p.$ 59.

		SECOND PART.
A1	1—2	Add "the dancers falling into one line (the three men below the three women)."
A2	1—2	Add "the dancers falling into one line (the three men above the three women)."

CONFESS. $p.$ 61.

		FIRST PART.
B1	5—8	First man turns second man once-and-a-half round ; simultaneously second and fourth women, and third and first women turn each other once round.

		THIRD PART.
B1	5—8	Add "once clockwise and once counter-clockwise in the middle of the ring formed by the women."
B2	5—8	Add "once clockwise and once counter-clockwise."

UPON A SUMMER'S DAY. $p.$ 71.

		FIRST PART.
B1	5—8	Substitute "(r.s.)" for "(sk.s.)."

BROOM, THE BONNY, BONNY BROOM. $p.$ 74.

		THIRD PART.
A3	1—4	Insert "with inside hands" after "left wall."

LULL ME BEYOND THEE. *p.* 79.

MUSIC.		MOVEMENTS.
		SECOND PART.
B2	1—4	First and third couples four abreast (third man on the left, third woman on the right) lead up a double and fall back a double; while second and fourth couples lead down a double and fall back a double (fourth man on the left, fourth woman on the right) (r.s.).

THE MERRY, MERRY MILKMAID. *p.* 83.

		FIRST PART.
B1	1—2	First man and first woman take two steps back, meet, and take both hands; while third man and third woman do the same.
B2	1—2	Second man and second woman take two steps back, meet and take both hands; while fourth man and fourth woman do the same.

THE PHŒNIX. *p.* 85.

Running-step throughout the dance.

IRISH TROT. *p.* 99.

		SECOND PART.
A1	Bar 2	For "slipping round clockwise" read "moving round clockwise (r.s.)."

ROW WELL. *p.* 102.

		SECOND PART.
A	5—8	First and second men go a single to the right and honour, and then change places, passing by the left; while first and second women do the same (progressive).

THE COUNTRY DANCE BOOK.—PART IV.

SELLENGER'S ROUND.   *p.* 40.

It is customary to conclude the dance with a repetition of the First Part.

HIT AND MISS.   *p.* 43.

Music.		Movements.
		Omit "*Running-step throughout the dance.*"
		First Part.
C	1—6	Add "(sk.s.)."

SCOTCH CAP.   *p.* 53.

		First Part.
B1	5—8	Omit "fall back two steps."
		Third Part.
B2	1—8	Add "giving left hands."

GREENWOOD.   *p.* 55.

		Fourth Part.
A3	1—8	Each file goes the whole-hey, second man facing first woman, and second woman facing third man, passing by the right.

STEP STATELY.   *p.* 58.

		Second Part.
B	5—8	Substitute "(r.s.)" for "(sk.s.)."
		Third Part.
A	5—6	The first three men taking hands, and the first three women doing the same, all fall back a double.
	7—8	The two files move forward a double, second and third men changing places with their partners, passing by the right.
		It is customary to conclude the dance with a repetition of the First Part.

THE HEALTH. *p.* 66.

Running-step throughout the dance.

EPSOM NEW WELLS. *p.* 75.

Music.	Movements.
A 1—4 & 5—8	Insert " with the right hand " after " half-way round " in each case.

A TRIP TO KILBURN. *p.* 79.

B2	For " $\left\{\begin{matrix}1—4\\5—8\end{matrix}\right\}$ " read " 1—8."

MY LADY WINWOOD'S MAGGOT. *p.* 80.

B2	For " $\left\{\begin{matrix}1—4\\5—8\end{matrix}\right\}$ " read " 1—8."

MR. ISAAC'S MAGGOT. *p.* 84.

B 5—8	First and second couples circular-hey, three changes, partners facing. All four face up in line, first man and first woman standing between second man and second woman.

THE MARY AND DOROTHY. *p.* 96.

B 1—4	Insert " with inside hands " after " down the middle."